Fourth Workshop on Teaching Natural Language Processing 2013

Sofia, Bulgaria
9 August 2013

ISBN: 978-1-62748-984-3

Printed from e-media with permission by:

Curran Associates, Inc.
57 Morehouse Lane
Red Hook, NY 12571

Some format issues inherent in the e-media version may also appear in this print version.

Printed by Curran Associates, Inc. (2013)

For permission requests, please contact the Association for Computational Linguistics at the address below.

Association for Computational Linguistics
209 N. Eighth Street
Stroudsburg, Pennsylvania 18360

Phone: 1-570-476-8006
Fax: 1-570-476-0860

acl@aclweb.org

Additional copies of this publication are available from:

Curran Associates, Inc.
57 Morehouse Lane
Red Hook, NY 12571 USA
Phone: 845-758-0400
Fax: 845-758-2634
Email: curran@proceedings.com
Web: www.proceedings.com

ACL 2013

51st Annual Meeting of the Association for Computational Linguistics

Proceedings of the Fourth Workshop on Teaching Natural Language Processing

August 9, 2013
Sofia, Bulgaria

Preface

Welcome to the Fourth Workshop on Teaching Natural Language Processing. Following the first three very successful ACL workshops on issues in teaching computational linguistics and natural language processing (in 2002, 2005 and 2008, `http://www.teachingnlp.org`), we meet together again to discuss the recent advances in educational tools and methodologies for this field and our contributors' experience with novel assignments, targeting various student populations, and integrating the teaching of computational linguistics into other courses and classroom activities.

In view of the fact that this year's ACL is held in Bulgaria, the second country (after the Soviet Union) to introduce linguistic Olympiads for secondary school students as a way of acquainting them and the general public with the science of language and the associated applied areas, this workshop has a special focus on Olympiads in linguistics and especially computational linguistics. We will talk about the basics, the composition of problems, the experience of some countries that have joined the linguistic Olympic community relatively recently and of the challenges of the young but dynamic International Linguistics Olympiad.

We will discuss how computational linguistic problems illustrate fundamental or applied issues in natural language processing, rather than individual languages or linguistic theory. Although this variety of the self-sufficient linguistic problem has always had a presence at linguistic contests, in the US and the other Anglophone countries it has become a primary feature, and its development is of eminent interest.

In addition to six papers in the special section on Olympiads in (Computational) Linguistics and seven in the general one on Teaching Natural Language Processing, the program of the workshop includes two panels.

We thank all authors who submitted papers to the workshop as well as the members of the program committee and the panelists.

Ivan Derzhanski and Dragomir Radev, workshop co-chairs

Organizers:

Ivan Derzhanski, Bulgarian Academy of Sciences
Dragomir Radev, University of Michigan

Program Committee:

Steven Abney, University of Michigan
Jason Eisner, Johns Hopkins University
Dominique Estival, University of Western Sydney
Dick Hudson, University College London
Boris Iomdin, Russian Academy of Sciences
Ben King, University of Michigan
Zornitsa Kozareva, USC/ISI
Lori Levin, Carnegie Mellon University
Patrick Littell, University of British Columbia
Deryle Lonsdale, Brigham Young University
Rada Mihalcea, University of North Texas
Vincent Ng, University of Texas, Dallas
James Pustejovsky, Brandeis University
Harold Somers, All Ireland Linguistics Olympiad

Table of Contents

Conference Program
(Morning)

9:00-9:10 **Welcome**

9:10-10:30 **Olympiads - PAPERS I (4 long papers)**

(9:10-9:30) *Rosetta Stone Linguistic Problems*
Bozhidar Bozhanov and Ivan Derzhanski

(9:30-9:50) *Linguistic Problems Based on Text Corpora*
Boris Iomdin, Alexander Piperski and Anton Somin

(9:50-10:10) *Introducing Computational Concepts in a Linguistic Olympiad*
Patrick Littell, Lori Levin, Jason Eisner and Dragomir Radev

(10:10-10:30) *Multilingual Editing of Linguistic Problems*
Ivan Derzhanski

11:00-11:30 **Olympiads - PAPERS II (1 long paper + 1 short paper)**

(11:00-11:20) *Learning from OzCLO, the Australian Computational and Linguistics Olympiad*
Dominique Estival, John Henderson, Mary Laughren, Diego Mollá, Cathy Bow, Rachel Nordlinger, Verna Rieschild, Andrea C. Schalley, Alexander W. Stanley and Colette Mrowa-Hopkins

(11:20-11:30) *The Swedish Model of Public Outreach of Linguistics to secondary school Students through Olympiads*
Patrik Roos and Hedvig Skirgård

11:30-12:30 **Olympiads - PANEL**

Conference Program
(Afternoon)

14:00-15:40 **Teaching NLP and CL - PAPERS (4 short papers + 3 long papers)**

(14:00-14:10) *Correspondence Seminar: Bringing Linguistics to High Schools*
Matěj Korvas and Vojtěch Diatka

(14:10-14:20) *Artificial IntelliDance: Teaching Machine Learning through a Choreography*
Apoorv Agarwal and Caitlin Trainor

(14:20-14:30) *Treebanking for Data-driven Research in the Classroom*
John Lee, Ying Cheuk Hui and Yin Hei Kong

(14:30-14:40) *Learning Computational Linguistics through NLP Evaluation Events: the experience of Russian evaluation initiative*
Anastasia Bonch-Osmolovskaya, Svetlana Toldova and Olga Lyashevskaya

(14:40-15:00) *A Virtual Manipulative for Learning Log-Linear Models*
Francis Ferraro and Jason Eisner

(15:00-15:20) *Teaching the Basics of NLP and ML in an Introductory Course to Information Science*
Apoorv Agarwal

(15:20-15:40) *Semantic Technologies in IBM Watson*
Alfio Gliozzo, Or Biran, Siddharth Patwardhan and Kathleen McKeown

16:00-17:30 **Teaching NLP and CL - PANEL**

Rosetta Stone Linguistic Problems

Bozhidar Bozhanov
Problem Committee
International Linguistics Olympiad
bozhidar.bozhanov@gmail.com

Ivan Derzhanski
Problem Committee
International Linguistics Olympiad
iad58g@gmail.com

Abstract

This paper describes the process of composing problems that are suitable for competitions in linguistics. The type of problems described is "Rosetta Stone"—a bilingual problem where typically one of the languages is unknown, and the other is the native language of the person solving the problem. The process includes selecting phenomena, composing and arranging the data and assignments in order to illustrate the phenomena, and verifying the solvability and complexity of the problem.

1 Introduction

1.1 What is a linguistic problem?

Linguistic problems are a genre of composition that presents linguistic facts and phenomena in enigmatic form (Derzhanski, Payne 2009). As an entertaining way of learning about language(s) and linguistics, they are suitable for a general audience (witness their occasional appearance in popular science journals, e.g., *Nauka i zhizn'* 1980.10, 2012.6) and can also be useful in the classroom or in linguistic textbooks as illustrations or exercises for the reader (cf., e.g., Testelets 2001), but at present their most common purpose is to be assigned to (usually) secondary-school students at contests such as the Moscow Traditional Olympiad in Linguistics, the North American Computational Linguistics Olympiad or the International Linguistics Olympiad (IOL).

Each problem may present phenomena from one or several subfields of the study of language—phonology, morphology, syntax, semantics, historical and comparative linguistics, writing systems, pragmatics, discourse analysis, etc.

There are two important requirements of the genre:

- The problem must be self-sufficient: it should contain all the necessary information for its solving, not expecting from the solver any prior knowledge (of languages, linguistics, mathematics, etc.) beyond what is commonly included into the secondary school curriculum.
- The problem must be unambiguous: it should not allow more than one plausible explanation of the data.

1.2 What is a "Rosetta Stone" linguistic problem?

In a "Rosetta Stone" linguistic problem[1] the material has the form of ordered matching expressions of two languages or language-like symbolic systems, so chosen as to enable deducing the regularities behind the correspondences, which is the essence of the problem.

In the most common subtype of Rosetta Stone the solver is given expressions (words, phrases, sentences) in an unfamiliar language and their translations into "Solverese" (a familiar working language, usually the solver's native language)[2] and, in most cases, asked to translate more expressions in both directions (from the unfamiliar language to Solverese and *vice versa*). Less often the assignments require one to choose translations from a list, produce alternative transla-

[1] This term was introduced by Ivan Derzhanski in 2004 and gained currency within IOL's Problem Committee. The idea is that the way to solve such a problem (by comparing matching structures in different languages) resembles Jean-François Champollion's method of deciphering Ancient Egyptian with the aid of a parallel Egyptian and Greek text inscribed on a granodiorite stele that had been discovered near the town of Rashid (Rosetta) in the Nile Delta. Another term for this type of problem is *bilingua*, used by the team of the Moscow Linguistic Olympiad.

[2] This term was also invented by Ivan Derzhanski in 2008 and became part of the jargon of the Problem Committee of IOL. It is modelled upon language names such as *Chinese*, but is also inspired by *Motherese* 'speech used by adults when talking to infants' and similar coinages.

IOL1		IOL2		IOL3		IOL4		IOL5	
®4	**15.24**	**®1**	**15.26**	**®1**	**12.90**	**®1**	**12.63**	#5	14.62
#1	14.85	#4	15.17	#2	11.98	#2	9.17	#2	14.17
#5	14.06	#2	11.78	**®4**	**11.56**	**®5**	**8.81**	#1	11.80
#3	11.56	#5	8.87	**®3**	**10.66**	**®4**	**8.77**	#4	3.80
#2	6.88	#3	3.85	#5	4.84	#3	6.79	#3	3.43
IOL6		IOL7		IOL8		IOL9		IOL10	
®4	**13.00**	**®1**	**14.77**	#1	15.49	**®3**	**13.62**	**®5**	**9.60**
#3	12.96	#2	11.29	#3	14.29	#2	9.13	**®4**	**8.92**
#1	12.94	**®5**	**9.28**	#4	9.55	**®1**	**6.38**	**®2**	**7.69**
®5	**9.78**	#3	4.38	#5	9.43	#4	4.75	**®1**	**6.41**
#2	5.75	#4	1.33	#2	7.38	#5	4.64	#3	6.29

Table 1. IOL1–10: the average scores for the problems (ordered from highest to lowest).

tions, judge the well-formedness of phrases or sentences in the unknown language, locate errors, or explain the meanings of words or phrases that don't translate readily into Solverese.

If the material of the unfamiliar language consists of number names, their meanings can be given in figures instead of Solverese expressions. Problems on number names are often thought to form a separate type, but arguably (Zhurinsky 1993; Derzhanski 2007) they are ordinary problems on a somewhat peculiar discrete domain of semantics.

As such, Rosetta Stones contrast with "Chaos and Order" problems, in which the expressions in the two languages are not ordered and matching them is part of the solution, or problems on inferring the laws of a single system (a fragment of a language's grammar, a poetic genre, a mnemonic system) without comparing it to another.

In all cases solving the problem involves discovering and analysing the regular correspondences and deriving a mini-grammar and vocabulary of the unfamiliar language from the data before proceeding to the assignments.

The genre described above is the bread-and-butter type of problem at linguistic contests. Although the classification of a linguistic problem is often a fuzzy issue, among the 50 problems that have been assigned at the individual contests of the first ten instalments of IOL, 18 (36%) can be counted as classical Rosetta Stones, as are eight (40%) of the 20 problems in (Derzhanski 2009). Not surprisingly, experienced solvers are better prepared to handle these than problems of other types: at all eight IOLs where such problems were assigned, the best-solved problem was always one of them, and the worst-solved problem never was one. This can be seen in Table 1, which presents the contestants' average scores for the problems of IOL1–10, ordered from highest to lowest within each year, with the classical Rosetta Stones marked by "®" and boldface. (The maximal possible score for each problem was 20. There were two exceptions at IOL1, but in the table the scores for those problems have been normalised to enable comparison with the others.) Or it can be observed that none of the ten worst-solved problems at IOL1–10 have been classical Rosetta Stones, whilst among the 40 others they are evenly distributed, meaning that they are relatively well received, but not trivially easy.

Some increasingly non-prototypical subtypes of Rosetta Stones include problems in which:

- the unfamiliar language is not a speakable human language but a symbolic system such as a pasigraphy (e.g., Linzbach's "Transcendental Algebra"[3]);
- or the two matching sets of data are not expressions in an unfamiliar language and in Solverese but expressions in two unfamiliar languages;
- or they are words or sentences of a single language written in two scripts, or in orthography and a transcription, and one has to derive the rules of spelling and pronunciation;
- or they are cognate words (or loanwords and their sources) of two languages or dialects, and the rules to derive are phonetic correspondences;
- or both sets are non-language data which, however, share some important characteristics with human language and thus can be said to be of linguistic interest

[3] IOL1, problem 1 (Ksenia Gilyarova).

(e.g., messenger RNA sequences and the corresponding polypeptide chains[4]).

In some problems there are more than two languages (or language-like systems) involved: the data may consist of parallel sentences in two unfamiliar languages and in Solverese, or in an unfamiliar language in two scripts (or in orthography and transcription) as well as Solverese[5], or of cognate words of several languages.

With the concept so extended, the ratio of Rosetta Stones at the first ten IOLs rises to more than a half (27 of 50). However, although all subtypes of Rosetta Stone share the same general method, all are not equal in linguistic content. What follows will concentrate on the classical subtype.

2 Selecting phenomena

Like most other types of problems, a Rosetta Stone problem is normally built around an interesting linguistic phenomenon that is not present in Solverese.[6] In order to illustrate that phenomenon, some side phenomena must be included which allow forming actual sentences, phrases, or word forms.

It is characteristic of the classical subtype of Rosetta Stone that the Solverese expressions are given for the sake of their meaning only, so the bilingual analysis involves matching components of the *structure* of each expression in the unknown language with components of the *meaning* of its translation. Overestimating the importance of the structure of the Solverese (and treating the unfamiliar language as a code for Solverese) is an error frequently made even by experts in the field. Thus solving a problem of this type always involves some amount of semantic analysis of the Solverese expressions.

2.1 The main phenomenon

Having a single main phenomenon in a problem is not a rule—there may be two of them—but having more usually makes the problem too hard to solve in a limited timeframe. The main phenomenon is usually something interesting and intriguing that the author of the problem has stumbled upon while researching (or sometimes authoring, typically on the basis of fieldwork) a description of the unfamiliar language.

Some phenomena pertain to the ways in which the unfamiliar language expresses information that is also present in the translations (though likely not in the same form), others do not. Here are some examples of the former:

- semantically determined noun classes;
- ergativity (and split ergativity);
- direct–inverse argument marking;
- obviative (fourth person);
- overcounting in numerals.

The latter include phonological processes such as distant assimilation or dissimilation and sandhi, as well as complex allophony and allomorphy.

Sometimes a problem illustrates variation, i.e., is built on the fact that a class of Solverese expressions can be translated in more than one way into the unfamiliar language (which may or may not reflect an ambiguity of Solverese that is resolved there), or *vice versa* (in such case the data are often introduced as Solverese expressions with their translations into the other language).

2.2 The side phenomena

Side phenomena are included in order to properly construct examples that demonstrate the main phenomenon and to achieve the desired level of complexity. As a rule they are of lesser interest than the main phenomenon, but still require deducing from the data. They often concern such things as:

- word order;
- agreement;
- number or case marking;
- person and number marking;
- marking of verb tense and mood;
- relatively straightforward allomorphy.

The side phenomena can vary in difficulty. Some may be trivial (e.g., a plural affix) and some may be harder to discover (e.g., assimilation). There is no strict distinction between main and side phenomena. For example, assimilation may be a main phenomenon in a simpler problem and a side phenomenon in a more complex one.

The author should balance the number of the side phenomena: too few may make the main phenomenon too conspicuous and the problem too easy; too many may obscure the main phenomenon.

---

[4] IOL8, problem 4 (Alexander Berdichevsky).

[5] As in Champollion's original Rosetta Stone, which was in fact a *trilingua*, featuring Ancient Egyptian in hieroglyphic and demotic script as well as Greek.

[6] In the case of a problem intended for a multilingual contest such as IOL, this means that the main phenomenon must be absent from all working languages which will be used at the current instalment. With respect to the side phenomena this requirement is relaxed.

3 Constructing the data

The data in a problem is the language material (word forms, phrases or sentences) that is fully given to the solver—in the unfamiliar language and in Solverese. This material must represent all the chosen phenomena without any unaccountable exceptions.

For a phenomenon to be unambiguously discoverable, it must be illustrated by several examples in the data. The bare minimum, sufficient for simpler side phenomena, is two; the main phenomenon takes more. A statistical measure of the sufficiency of the material is developed in (Testelets 1994), but to the best of our knowledge neither this theoretical method nor any other is applied in practice to evaluate the quality of new problems.

3.1 Techniques for constructing the data

Here is a non-exhaustive list of frequently used techniques and approaches to constructing the data:

- Preselect a number of words that are usable in the problem—i.e., meet the requirements for representing the phenomena. For instance, if the phenomenon involves direct vs. indirect objects, transitive verbs will be needed.
- Make a table (or tables) of all possible forms of the chosen words that can appear in the problem, and choose some for the data, leaving some for the assignments.
- Group the words you have preselected according to their properties. For example, put stems ending in vowels and in consonants in separate groups if the suffixes depend on the final sound.
- If working with phrases or sentences, don't focus on the meaning. In general, it is sufficient if they aren't so absurd as to confuse the solver.
- Consider using assignments on translation from the unfamiliar language to Solverese to complement the data in showing that certain forms are possible.

This process often requires extensive search in dictionaries and work with reference grammars or informants (the latter is very desirable, but seldom done, for practical reasons).

Simplifying the grammatical patterns of the language or changing them in any other way is considered impermissible, but some parts may be concealed in order to make certain regular portions stand out.

3.2 The size of the dataset

There is no strict requirement for the number of examples presented to the solver. There have been problems with as few as 4 given sentences and as many as 25 word forms. The main factor to consider is phenomenon density. If the author can properly illustrate all the selected phenomena in a couple of sentences, then the number of examples is low, but the phenomenon density is high. Contrariwise, if an example may contain only a single instance of one of the phenomena, then the density is low, and many examples are required.

3.3 Parasitic solutions

A parasitic solution is one that correctly and plausibly accounts for the data in the problem but differs from the fact of the language. Although the plausibility of a parasitic solution can sometimes be a matter of debate, in general it indicates a flaw of the problem. If discovered by test-solving the problem, it can be blocked, usually by adding a specific example which it does not account for.

For example, a problem on split ergativity in Inuktitut[7] had an early version which allowed one to think that the ergative construction was used whenever the verb begins with a vowel (whereas in fact its use is triggered by semantic properties of the object). That would have been an unlikely explanation, but as pointed out in Section 1 the solver is not expected to possess linguistic proficiency and may not be able to tell a plausible hypothesis from an implausible one. Therefore an example was added where an ergative construction was used with a verb starting with a consonant. In that way the parasitic solution was no longer accounted for the data.

3.4 Scrambling the data

If the complexity of a Rosetta Stone problem is deemed insufficient, it may be increased by scrambling the data, that is, presenting the material without indicating which Solverese expression corresponds to each expression of the unfamiliar language. In this way the Rosetta Stone problem is turned into a problem of another type, Chaos and Order. Chaos and Order problems are beyond the scope of this article, so suffice it to say here that the prevailing expert opinion is that

[7] IOL6, problem 5 (Bozhidar Bozhanov).

this technique should be reserved for occasions where the possibility of presenting a phenomenon as a problem depends on it, and not used for adding mere technical complexity to an easy Rosetta Stone (section 6.1).

4 Constructing the assignments

The assignments are exercises on using the rules that the solver is expected to have deduced from the data. Their purpose is to verify that this has been done correctly, which is why they must not be doable by using simple analogy with the data; they must ask the solver to construct forms (or combinations of forms) that have not been given previously. Sometimes the assignments include more explicit material that will be used in them but could not have been given in the data. For example, if the data has the form of sentences and one of the phenomena is that the semantics of a noun determines its class which in turn determines the choice of an obligatory article, the assignments may include a short list of nouns in citation form for the solver to classify and use in translations (including them in the data would have revealed the articles).

As noted before, an assignment on translating from the unknown language to Solverese may also be used as a way of showing more examples of some phenomenon, thus reducing the number of examples required in the data. Any sentences (or phrases) assigned for translation from the unknown language should, however, be reasonably intuitive; an improbable translation may cause the solver to unduly question the rules.[8]

As also noted, apart from the most common "translate from X to Y" assignments, there can be assignments of other, less common types. This usually happens when the understanding of the main phenomenon is hard to assess only on the basis of translations. Questions of the form "Can you translate the following? If so, how? If not, why not?" may be asked, or an additional "story" may be told, with new pairs of matching explanations presented, especially if the phenomenon is a complex one and should be deduced in parts. Of course, formulations should be kept as simple as possible.

[8] A sentence meaning 'The dog shot itself' was nearly assigned for translation from Inuktitut into Solverese in IOL6, problem 5 (Bozhidar Bozhanov), but was eliminated in the final version.

5 Auxiliary information

Apart from data and assignments, a problem nearly always contains an introductory text, and frequently notes as well. Both may contain valuable information about the data or hints to the solver.

5.1 Introductory text

In most cases this is a mere cliché such as "Here are sentences in Such-and-Such language and their translations", also indicating whether the translations are ordered or scrambled and sometimes making other useful statements, e.g., that certain parts of the data are there for completeness but can be ignored when solving the problem, that the transcription has been simplified, etc. Such statements are usually made directly; it is not common for information to be expressed in this text in oblique ways.

5.2 Notes

In most cases notes (footnotes or endnotes) contain information on the language and descriptions of unknown sounds, and sometimes also explanations of unfamiliar concepts.

The information about the language usually contains taxonomy information, locality and number of speakers, for the solver's edification and for putting the problem in context. It is rarely useful for solving the problem.[9]

If the note mentions unfamiliar sounds (or spellings), it may do one of the following:

- simply state that these are sounds of the featured language, as a way of saying that they (or the letters used to write them) should be distinguished from others (and as a hint that their precise phonetic value is immaterial);
- give rough approximations to familiar sounds, usually with the only purpose of making it easier to read the problem

[9] The popular notion that the solver should strive to use independently acquired knowledge about language families in order to guess what phenomena may be present in the problem is at variance with the principle of self-sufficiency: information that is neither part of the problem nor common knowledge is as likely to be harmful as to be beneficial. On the other hand, the author may expect the reader to apply, for example, some generally known fact of geography along with the information from the note on where the language is spoken in order to deduce something about its lexicon.

(many people find it easier to handle words if they have some idea as to what they sound like);
- explain the phonetic characteristics of the sounds, often (though not always) to indicate a phonological phenomenon.

6 Assessing the complexity of the problem

As was said above, there is no objective way of assessing the complexity of a problem; test-solving is the only procedure. However, one can try to estimate the complexity on the basis of the triviality or obscurity of the main phenomenon, the number of side phenomena, and the quantity of the assignments. This can put the problem into the broad categories of "easy", "medium" and "hard".

The assessment of complexity is needed, first, in order to choose an appropriate forum and audience for the problem, and second, to design a scoring system if it is to be used at a competition where the scoring must be devised *a priori*. As a rule, finding the main phenomenon is harder than finding any of the side phenomena, and translating from the unfamiliar language is easier than translating into it.

6.1 Types of complexity

There are two types of complexity of a problem—linguistic complexity and technical complexity.

The former is the complexity related to figuring out the linguistic phenomena and deducing the grammar—grouping the examples into categories, determining the structure of the sentences, segmenting the word forms into morphemes, identifying phonological processes, etc.

The latter is about the technical complexity of doing the above and involves mechanical or logical tasks rather than linguistic ones. For example, unscrambling translations given out of order (a stage of solving Chaos and Order problems) is a purely technical task, done on the basis of the number of occurrences of the instances of the phenomena. This type of complexity simply makes the problem harder without adding anything linguistically interesting to it.

In a problem linguistic complexity is favoured upon technical complexity. Rosetta Stone problems rarely exhibit undesirable amounts of technical complexity, and this is one of the reasons for which they are the dominant type of problems at contests.

6.2 Specifics of scoring

Designing a scoring scheme is a process separate from composing the problem (in most cases the author doesn't even know at what contest the problem will be used and what the scoring system will be there, nor has any control over it; different contests seldom score a problem in the same way). In the case of a Rosetta Stone points may be allocated for finding the phenomena (as a rule, more for the main one and fewer for the side ones), as well as the assignments (reflecting an assessment of their relative importance and complexity). A study of the point counts won by the participants in the first ten instalments of IOL shows that, while on the average for each problem about ¼ of all contestants had scores in the middle third of the actual range and the rest were equally divided between high and low scorers, for classical Rosetta Stones the middle scorers outweighed the low ones. Table 2 presents the ratio of high to middle to low scorers for each problem, again with the classical Rosetta Stones marked by "®" and boldface.

IOL1		IOL2		IOL3		IOL4		IOL5	
#1	52:33:15	**®1**	**70:17:13**	**®1**	**58:26:16**	**®1**	**61:24:16**	#1	49:13:38
#2	24:03:73	#2	57:24:20	#2	54:10:36	#2	27:37:35	#2	66:28:07
#3	56:16:28	#3	09:09:83	**®3**	**48:16:36**	#3	24:25:51	#3	10:11:79
®4	**67:27:06**	#4	61:17:22	**®4**	**40:44:16**	**®4**	**18:49:33**	#4	15:02:84
#5	73:06:21	#5	04:36:60	#5	22:06:72	**®5**	**27:27:45**	#5	52:30:18
IOL6		**IOL7**		**IOL8**		**IOL9**		**IOL10**	
#1	55:34:10	**®1**	**67:23:09**	#1	76:18:06	**®1**	**18:38:43**	**®1**	**13:31:56**
#2	19:16:64	#2	45:27:28	#2	32:08:60	#2	23:38:38	**®2**	**36:13:51**
#3	60:27:13	#3	20:05:76	#3	69:23:08	**®3**	**61:22:17**	#3	17:24:60
®4	**51:33:16**	#4	03:05:92	#4	45:07:47	#4	13:13:74	**®4**	**17:47:36**
®5	**30:39:31**	**®5**	**30:42:28**	#5	27:35:37	#5	06:22:72	**®5**	**37:47:16**

Table 2. IOL1–10: ratio of high:middle:low scorers for each problem.

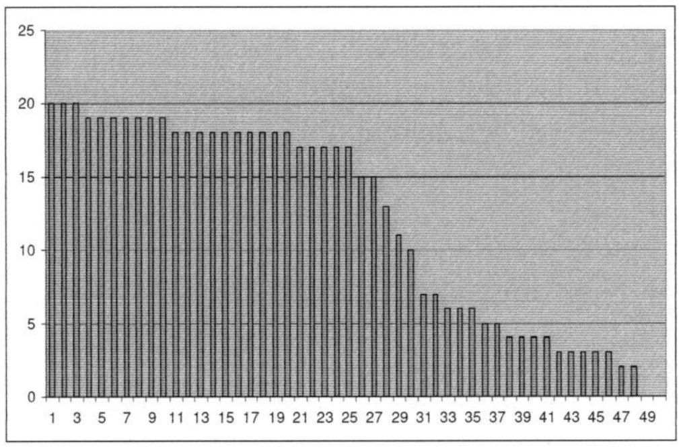

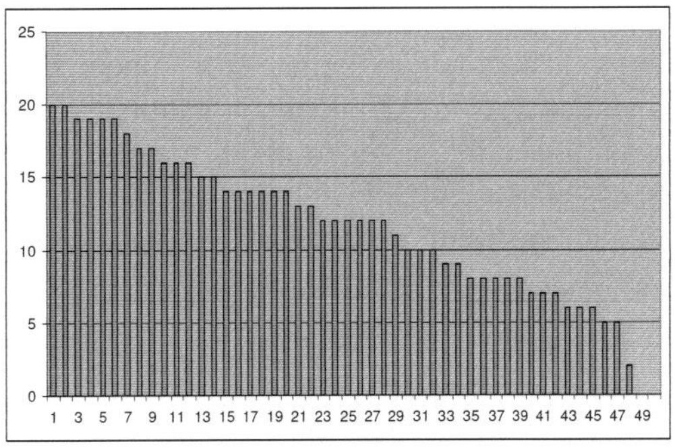

Figure 1. The distribution of scores for two IOL problems.

The reason for this is the inclusion of multiple phenomena. Finding a side phenomenon and using it in the assignments carries a portion of the points, even though the main phenomenon may not have been discovered; Rosetta Stones are almost never "all-or-none" problems.

This is an important factor when considering the complexity of a problem within a problem set. "All-or-none" problems create the danger of anomalies in the end results of a competition (contestants scoring lower than their abilities due to random factors) and of discouraging less experienced participants.

Figure 1 further illustrates the difference in the distribution of scores. The problem on the left was a Chaos and Order on Lango.[10] The one on the right was a classical Rosetta Stone on Yoruba.[11] The contestants' average scores for the two problems were extremely close (11.98 and 11.56, respectively), but the Rosetta Stone took less insight, though more work on the whole, and this made for a smoother ranking.

7 Co-authoring a problem

It is not uncommon for a problem to be authored by two people. This sometimes means that the authorship has been divided chronologically: one person wrote a problem that the other thoroughly revised (to an extent thought to amount to co-authorship). Or else they may have worked jointly on creating the problem from the idea and the original data, possibly dividing among themselves the tasks, which include (in the case of a Rosetta Stone problem) selecting side phenomena, selecting material, constructing the table of usable forms, and constructing assignments. This modularity of the authoring process greatly facilitates co-authoring.

The common-sense iterative procedure for collaborative work when the two authors are not physically present in one place and cannot hold discussions while constructing the problem (each author in turn making changes and sending them over to the other to review) has some specifics in this case—changes must be explicitly accounted for, so that one does not by accident remove an example that the other thought necessary for illustrating a phenomenon.

8 Problem approval process

When the problem is finished it has to go through an approval process before being used in competitions. The formality of the process depends on the contests and the rules of problem committee. Some steps are:

- Idea validation: not every language phenomenon can be used for a linguistic problem at all.
- Pretesting/beta-testing: no amount of reasoning can substitute for people's actual attempts to solve the problem, as a way of evaluating its difficulty and verifying its unambiguity.
- Assessing suitability for a given competition: a problem which is good in principle may be deemed unsuitable for a specific place or time. It may be too hard for an introductory round (or too easy for an advanced one), or it may contain phenomena that are very similar to ones used at a recent instalment of the same contest. If judged usable in principle but not momentarily, the problem may be put in a repository, where it is saved for future competitions.

This is a generic process that applies to all problem types, but some details are relevant specifically to Rosetta Stones.

[10] IOL3, problem 2 (Ksenia Gilyarova).
[11] IOL3, problem 4 (Ivan Derzhanski).

8.1 Beta-testing

The process of beta-testing is the most important step before finalising a problem. A solution (or non-solution) usually leads to modifications in the problem and a further version is released, which should be beta-tested again. Modifications carried out as result of test solutions include:

- blocking parasitic solutions;
- showing more examples of an under-represented phenomenon;
- removing or adding side phenomena in order to reduce or augment the complexity of the problem;
- amending assignments in order to prevent them from being doable by analogy with the data;
- clarifying assignments that are hard to understand.

The process continues until no more changes are required.

8.2 Translating problems

Linguistic problems have always been translated for a variety of purposes, from using problems made in one country at contests (or in lectures) in another through accommodating overseas guest competitors to running international contests. This is not always easy. The new Solverese may make some things less or more evident, it may share the main phenomenon with the featured language (which means that the problem ceases being a genuine problem in translation), or the solution may depend on recalling some facts of the original Solverese that are lost in translation. Often the choice is between an awkward wording and a problem that is not functionally equivalent to the original.[12] Which is preferable may depend on the occasion: an old foreign problem is worth translating and reusing only if it sounds natural in translation; it may be acceptable for guest participants in another country's national contest to be at a slight disadvantage, but at an international competition equality is crucial.

Rosetta Stone problems often involve phrases or sentences, which means that in principle they contain more opportunities for untranslatability. In light of this it may seem a paradox that they are so frequent at IOL. Yet it appears that problems of other types, and especially unclassifiable problems, are harder to make work equally well in several languages than Rosetta Stones are. The type wins out thanks to its familiarity.

9 Conclusion

Composing linguistic problems is a challenging task, which involves many steps and considerations. A good problem is unambiguous, contains well-presented interesting phenomena, does not have parasitic solutions and has prevailing linguistic complexity.

A Rosetta Stone problem enables authors to illustrate the most interesting linguistic phenomena, allows for smoothly distributed and fine-grained results and, as described above, has a relatively straightforward and well-defined composition workflow. No surprise, then, that it has become an expected feature at every linguistic contest.

References

Ivan A. Derzhanski. 2007. Mathematics in Linguistic Problems. In: L. Dimitrova and L. Pavlov (eds.), *Mathematical and Computational Linguistics. Jubilee International Conference, 6 July 2007*, Sofia, 49–52.

Ivan A. Derzhanski. 2009. *Linguistic Magic and Mystery*. Union of Bulgarian Mathematicians, Sofia.

Ivan A. Derzhanski and Thomas E. Payne. 2009. The Linguistics Olympiads: Academic competitions in linguistics for secondary school students. In: K. Denham and A. Lobeck (eds.), *Linguistics at School: Language Awareness in Primary and Secondary Education*, Cambridge University Press, Cambridge, UK, 213–226.

Yakov G. Testelets. 1994. Linguistic Problems and the "Presumption of the Author's Mildness". In: V.I. Belikov, E.V. Muravenko and N.V. Pertsov (resp. eds.), *Sign: A collection of papers on linguistics, semiotics and poetics* in memoriam *of A.N. Zhurinsky* (in Russian), Russian Educational Centre, Moscow, 213–224.

Yakov G. Testelets. 2001. *An Introduction to General Syntax* (in Russian). Russian State University for the Humanities, Moscow.

Alfred N. Zhurinsky. 1993. *Word, Letter, Number: A discussion of self-sufficient linguistic problems with an analysis of a hundred samples of the genre* (in Russian). Nauka, Moscow.

[12] This may happen, for instance, when translating glosses of sentences from Russian, which lacks articles, into a language that has them: if some nouns become definite and others indefinite, this will create a new opposition that the solver will have to consider.

Linguistic Problems Based on Text Corpora

Boris Iomdin
V.V. Vinogradov Institute of Russian Language, Russian Academy of Sciences (Moscow)
National Research University Higher School of Economics (Moscow, Russia)
iomdin@ruslang.ru

Alexander Piperski
M.V. Lomonosov Moscow State University (Moscow, Russia)
Russian State University for the Humanities (Moscow, Russia)
apiperski@gmail.com

Anton Somin
Russian State University for the Humanities (Moscow, Russia)
somin@tut.by

Abstract

The paper is focused on self-contained linguistic problems based on text corpora. We argue that corpus-based problems differ from traditional linguistic problems because they make it possible to represent language variation. Furthermore, they often require basic statistical thinking from the students. The practical value of using data obtained from text corpora for teaching linguistics through linguistic problems is shown.

1 Introduction

The genre of self-contained linguistic problems appeared long before the onset of corpus linguistics. The authors of most problems either constructed phrases or sentences on their own, or (much less commonly) used some real texts (e.g. excerpts from ancient manuscripts). Now that text corpora become widespread, they offer new possiblities for problem composing. This paper gives examples of such problems offered to high school students in Russia at recent linguistic olympiads. We comment on the ways such new problems are solved and show how the data obtained from text corpora and linguistic problems based thereon could be used for teaching linguistics to high school students.

We deliberately include some of the original Russian versions of the problems alongside with their English translations (made specially for this paper and never published before), so that (1) those familiar with the Russian language could use the problems for training, and (2) issues of linguistic problem translation could be illustrated, too: translations of linguistic problems are not always equivalent to the originals (cf. Derzhanski et al. 2004).

2 Corpus-based problems and traditional problems: what is the difference?

The most straightforward way of using corpora for composing problems is to find real-world examples of some linguistics phenomena. If the problem deals with a language other than its author's native tongue, it is preferable to constructing phrases or sentences (unfortunately, when experts or native speakers look at constructed data in the problems assigned at some earlier contests, they sometimes find it non-idiomatic, infelicitous or even ungrammatical). If the problem illustrates some phenomenon in the native language of its author, it is also preferable to use corpus examples, because they do not impose the author's introspection upon students.

Some corpus-based problems are quite different from traditional linguistic problems. Corpus data allow to present linguistic variation in a problem, which was difficult to do before the corpora era. It might be diachronic variation, register variation or some other kind of variation.

The traditional linguistic problems require a strictly deterministic way of thinking ("if this, then that"). However, in real life linguists often have to deal with statistical patterns, and this is where corpus linguistics comes into play. Problems based on corpus data may exemplify this approach.

3 Some corpus-based problems

3.1 Corpus examples illustrating a linguistic phenomenon in the solvers' native language

Problem #1 (composed by Boris Iomdin)

При изучении фраз с глаголом *предлагать* естественно выделять два типа употреблений этого глагола. Ниже приведены примеры обоих типов употреблений.

I

1. *Дядя Владимир предложил трактирщику его заменить и поторговать за него* (А. Левицкая);
2. *Ходил на вокзал, предлагал пассажирам помочь снести вещи* (А. Пантелеев);
3. *А Плахотников предложил стать моим руководителем и поделиться всем, что знал сам как опытнейший дрессировщик* (В. Запашный);
4. *Узнав, что друг его плохо себя чувствует <...>, Диккенс с трогательной заботливостью предлагает приехать и помочь ему в работе* (М. Шагинян);
5. *Ира оказалась очень чутким и отзывчивым человеком и сразу же предложила Евгению Александровичу переехать к нему и ухаживать за его полупарализованной матерью* (О. Демьянова).

II

6. *Встретивший его адъютант предложил ему располагаться и ждать* (К. Симонов);
7. *Предлагаем читателям разработать, изготовить и испытать такое приспособление* (Б. Синельников);
8. *Но пришла сестра и предложила уйти, дать ему отдохнуть* (Л. Бронтман);
9. *Он предложил мне дать в их издательство книжку стихов* (А. Городницкий);
10. *Ире как человеку чуткому и отзывчивому было тяжело смотреть на страдания любимого человека, и она предложила продать квартиру и переехать жить к ней* (О. Демьянова).

Задание 1. Объясните, чем различаются эти два типа употреблений.

Задание 2. К какому типу употреблений можно отнести следующие примеры:

11. *Он предложил Мижуеву дать денег на это дело, и Мижуев радостно согласился* (М. Арцыбашев);
12. *Через два дня позвонили со студии и предложили приехать и заключить договор* (Л. Вертинская);
13. *И вот дедушка Рахленко предлагает Кусиелу прогнать мерзавца приказчика и вместо него взять моего отца* (А. Рыбаков);
14. *Я предложила Ире помочь деньгами, но она сказала, что у них есть на жизнь* (З. Масленикова).

Если в каких-то случаях Вы считаете, что возможны оба ответа, укажите это. Поясните Ваше решение.

Задание 3. Что Вы можете сказать о следующем примере:

15. *Он даже предложил мне давать Юре уроки французского языка и платить за урок тарелкой супа* (В. Гроссман)?

English translation:

Looking at sentences with the Russian verb *predlagat'* 'to offer, to suggest', one finds out that it can be used in two different ways. Consider some examples for both (the Russian verb in question is replaced by a fictional English verb *to predle*):

I

1. *Uncle Vladimir* ***predled*** *the barman to replace him and to trade for him for a while* (A. Levitskaya);
2. *He used to come to the railway station and* ***predle*** *the passengers to carry their luggage* (A. Panteleev);
3. *Plakhotnikov* ***predled*** *to become my instructor and to share with me everything he knew as a very experienced animal tamer* (V. Zapashny);
4. *As soon as he learned that his friend was sick, Dickens, with a touching affection,* ***predles*** *to come and help him in his work* (M. Shaginyan);
5. *Ira appeared to be a very considerate and sympathetic person: right away she* ***predled*** *to Evgeny Alexandrovich to settle at his place and to take care of his half-paralyzed mother* (O. Demyanova).

II

6. *The aide-de-camp who met him* ***predled*** *him to sit down and wait* (K. Simonov);
7. *We* ***predle*** *the readers to work out, make and test such a device* (B. Sinel'nikov);
8. *But a nurse came and* ***predled*** *to leave, to give him some rest* (L. Brontman);
9. *He* ***predled*** *me to submit a verse book to their publishing house* (A. Gorodnitsky);
10. *Ira, as a considerate and sympathetic person, found it hard to watch how her beloved one was suffering, so she* ***predled*** *to sell the apartment and to settle with her* (O. Demyanova).

1. Explain the difference between the two usages of the verb.

2. Consider the following examples. What can you say about the ways the verb *to predle* is used in them?

11. *He* ***predled*** *Mizhuev to give money for the cause, and Mizhuev gladly agreed* (M. Artsybashev);
12. *After two days, someone called from the studio and* ***predled*** *to come and sign a contract* (L. Vertinskaya);
13. *So, old Rakhlenko* ***predles*** *Kusiel to kick out the villain clerk and to employ my father instead* (A. Rybakov);
14. *I* ***predled*** *Ira to assist financially, but she told me that they had enough for a living* (Z. Maslenikova).

If in some cases you believe that both answers are possible, give both and explain.

3. What can you say about the following example:

15. *He even* ***predled*** *me to give French lessons to Yura and to pay with a plate of soup for each lesson* (V. Grossman)?

Solution of Problem #1

It can be seen that the verb *predlagat'* (or the artificial English verb *to predle*) may govern two types of infinitives: subject infinitives, as in I, and object infinitives, as in II. These two types of usage may represent two different senses of the verb *predlagat'*, which could roughly be translated as 'to offer (to do something)' and 'to suggest (that someone else does something)'. The most interesting thing here is that in many cases it is quite hard to determine whether the infinitive refers to the subject or to the object. In fact, both answers are possible in all examples 11–14. Example (15) seems infelicitous: the author clearly meant that 'me' is to give lessons and 'he' is to pay. See (Iomdin & Iomdin 2011) for further discussion.

Comment

This problem does not differ much from traditional linguistic problems. The solvers are offered textual examples from their native language and are requested to analyze them. However, it is important that these examples are not constructed, which makes the problem more trustworthy. No solver can say "I don't use this verb this way!" because s/he is confronted with real-life examples.

Problem #2 (composed by Boris Iomdin)

Один лингвист попросил знакомого голландца, хорошо знающего русский язык, перевести на голландский несколько отрывков из литературных произведений. Его интересовало, какие глаголы голландец использует для перевода тех русских глаголов, которые в приведённых ниже цитатах подчёркнуты. Варианты, предложенные голландцем, указаны в скобках.

1) *За пустую бутылку охотно отдавали свои огромные тростниковые шляпы. Все у нас наменяли* **(krijgen)** *этих шляп* (И. Гончаров).

2) *И вот работяга, отработав 12-14 часов в смену, моет полы ночью за эти две папиросы табаку. И ещё считает за счастье – ведь на табак он выменяет* **(krijgen)** *хлеб* (В. Шаламов).

3) *Книжек я наменял* **(krijgen)** *у мужиков, на курево хотели, да бумага толстая* (Л. Леонов).

4) *Кондуктор того трамвая отнёс пальто на барахолку и там обменял* **(ruilen)** *на сметану, крупу и помидоры* (Д. Хармс).

5) *На пирожные он выменивал* **(ruilen)** *хлеб, муку, масло, пшено, табак – весь состав своего пайка, за исключением сахара: сахар он оставлял себе* (В. Ходасевич).

6) *Наменяли* **(krijgen)** *пятаков, полчаса дозванивались* (М. Веллер).

7) *Но если портному не нужна груша, а нужен, к примеру сказать, стол, то вы должны пойти к столяру, дать ему грушу за то, что он сделает стол, а потом этот стол выменять* **(ruilen)** *у портного на брюки* (Н. Носов).

8) *Но, как видно, руссы сильно желали выменивать* **(krijgen)** *на свои товары арабские монеты, диргемы, которые везде и во всяком значении имели большую ценность* (С. Соловьёв).

9) *Он бежал ночью из Дырок прямо на квартиру к Учителю, винтовку обменял* **(ruilen)** *на две бутылки самогона и в пьяном виде декламировал "Клеветникам России"* (И. Эренбург).

10) *Этот кальян выменял* **(krijgen)**, *или, правду сказать, выманил я у английского путешественника* (А. Бестужев-Марлинский).

11) *...Толпою окружённый слуг;*
Усердствуя, они в часы вина и драки
И честь и жизнь его не раз спасали: вдруг
На них он выменял **(krijgen)** *борзые три собаки!* (А. Грибоедов).

12) *Я сегодня, гражданин,*
Плохо спал:
Душу я на керосин
Обменял **(ruilen)** (В. Зоргенфрей).

Задание 1. Дано ещё несколько цитат. Определите, какие глаголы использовал голландец для перевода каждого из подчёркнутых глаголов. Если в каких-то случаях Вы не можете выполнить задание с уверенностью, отметьте это. Поясните Ваше решение.

А. *В доме было уже продано, выменяно на продукты всё, что можно. Кроме пианино* (И. Грекова).

Б. *Вот он сидит за большим столом и кладёт резолюции на подносимых бумагах: "От-ка-*

зать!!!" Вы хотите обменять *что-то меньшее на что-то большее. Отказать! Вы хотите* обменять *что-то большее на что-то меньшее. Отказать!* (В. Войнович).

В. *Выменять ножик на удочку* (С. Ожегов, Н. Шведова, Толковый словарь русского языка).

Г. *Он два дня не ел хлеба, затем* выменял *на хлеб большой фибровый чемодан* (В. Шаламов).

Д. *Теперь следует вопрос: как добывали руссы свои северные товары? Конечно, они могли* выменивать *их у туземцев на какие-нибудь произведения греческой промышленности...; но главным источником приобретения были дани и потом охота* (С. Соловьёв).

Е. *Я, наверное, не зря*
В этот раз ходил в моря,
Наменял *я там подарков,*
Ждёт их вся моя родня (О. Газманов).

Задание 2. Опираясь на материал задачи, сформулируйте правила употребления голландских глаголов *krijgen* и *ruilen*.

English translation:

A linguist asked a speaker of Dutch familiar with the Russian language to translate several excerpts from Russian books into Dutch. He was interested in the verbs the Dutch speaker would use as equivalents for certain Russian verbs: *namenjat'* (hereafter 'to N'), *obmenjat'* (hereafter 'to O') and *vymenjat'* (hereafter 'to V'), all associated with the idea of exchange. The equivalents used by the Dutch speaker are given in brackets.

1. *They were willing to give away their enormous reed hats for an empty bottle. We all N-ed* **(krijgen)** *these hats* (I. Goncharov).
2. *So the drudge, having worked for 12 to 14 hours in a shift, washes the floors during the night for these two cigarettes. And he even is happy with it, since he will V* **(krijgen)** *bread for the tobacco* (V. Shalamov).
3. *I N-ed* **(krijgen)** *some books from the peasants, they wanted to use them for smoking, but the paper's too thick* (L. Leonov).
4. *The tram conductor took the coat to the flea market and there he O-ed* **(ruilen)** *it for sour cream, groats and tomatoes* (D. Kharms).
5. *For pastry he V-ed* **(ruilen)** *bread, flour, butter, millet, tobacco, – all his ration, except for sugar, which he always kept* (V. Khodasevich).
6. *They N-ed* **(krijgen)** *five kopeck coins and tried to establish a telephone connection for half an hour* (M. Veller).
7. *But if the tailor does not need pears, but needs a table for example, then you have to go to the woodworker, give him a pear for the table he should make, and then V* **(ruilen)** *this table for trousers with the tailor* (N. Nosov).
8. *But apparently the Russians really wished to V* **(krijgen)** *for their goods Arabian coins, dirhem, which had a great value everywhere* (S. Solovyov).
9. *At night, he ran away from the Holes directly to the Teacher's apartment, O-ed* **(ruilen)** *the gun for two bottles of alkie, and being drunk recited "To the slanderers of Russia"* (I. Erenburg).
10. *I V-ed* **(krijgen)**, *or, to say the truth, juggled out this water-pipe from a British traveler* (A. Bestuzhev-Marlinsky).
11. *Had a team of loyal servants / That during fight-and-drinking rounds / Had saved his life and honour, but then once / He suddenly V-ed* **(krijgen)** *them for three hounds.* (A. Griboyedov, translation by A. Vagapov)
12. *Today I slept bad, citizen: I O-ed* **(ruilen)** *my soul for kerosene* (V. Sorgenfrei).

1. Consider some more examples. Determine which verbs the Dutch speaker would use in these examples. If in some cases you believe several solutions are possible, explain.

A. *In the house, everything was already sold,* V-ed *for food. Except for the piano* (I. Grekova).

B. *Here is he sitting at a large table, writing his decisions on the documents he is given: "Refu-sal!!!" You want to* O *something smaller for something larger. Refusal! You want to* O *something larger for something smaller. Refusal!* (V. Voynovich).

C. V *a knife for a fishing rod* (Ozhegov and Shvedova Explanatory Dictionary).

D. *For two days, he had not been eating bread, and then he* V-ed *for bread a large wooden chest* (V. Shalamov).

E. *Now comes a question: how did the Russians get their Northern goods? Of course they could* V *them from the locals for some Greek manufactured goods ...; but the main source for them were imposts, and then hunting* (S. Solovyev).

F. *Probably not in vain / Was I at sea this time / I* N-ed *presents there, / And my whole family is waiting for them* (O. Gazmanov).

2. Based on the data in the problem, explain what the Dutch verbs *krijgen* and *ruilen* mean.

Solution of Problem #2

All three verbs in question are used with objects. With N (*namenjat'*), the object always signifies the thing obtained in the exchange; with O (*obmenjat'*), the object always signifies the thing given away in the exchange. As for V (*vymenjat'*), it is used in both ways (which is a very rare case of a double government pattern). The Dutch verb *krijgen*, therefore, means 'to get in return', and *ruilen* means 'to give away'.

Comment

This problem is similar to problem #1 in the way it exploits corpus data., The examples come from real texts (and even the Dutch speaker is real), and the only difference is the reference to a foreign language which makes it easier to see the different senses of the words in the solvers' native language.

3.2 Corpus examples illustrating diachronic variation

Problem #3 (composed by Boris Iomdin)

Слово *параллельно* в литературном языке может управлять как существительными в дательном падеже (конструкция А), так и существительными в творительном падеже с предлогом *с* (конструкция Б). Ниже даны примеры обеих конструкций:

1. *Васич увидел лощинку. Она шла* ***параллельно*** *немцам, преграждала им путь к дивизиону* (Г. Бакланов).
2. *Её путь лежал* ***параллельно*** *маршруту трамвая* (Б. Пастернак).
3. *Мне было неприятно, что какие-то люди* ***параллельно*** *с нами, по обе стороны от нас, пробираются на холм* (Ф. Искандер).
4. *Теперь они шли* ***параллельно*** *насыпи* (А. и Б. Стругацкие).
5. *Наматывая мили на кардан, / Я еду* ***параллельно*** *проводам* (В. Высоцкий, 1971).
6. *Намечались короткие летние, перед отпуском, гастроли в Риге* ***параллельно*** *с работой двух московских сцен* (С. Пилявская).
7. *Новые восьми-девятиэтажные дома стояли разомкнутым строем* ***параллельно*** *бульвару* (Ю. Даниэль).
8. *Отросший ус торчал уже не* ***параллельно*** *земной поверхности, а почти перпендикулярно, как у пожилого кота* (И. Ильф, Е. Петров).
9. *Мы глядели на некоторые беседки и храмы по высотам, любовались длинною, идущею* ***параллельно*** *с берегом кедровою аллеею* (И. Гончаров).
10. ***Параллельно*** *с монтажом идёт и отделка фасада* («Комсомольская правда»).
11. *С каждым годом заводскому населению приходится тяжелее, а* ***параллельно*** *с этим возвышается благосостояние правителей, управляющих, поверенных и целого сонма служащего люда* (Д. Мамин-Сибиряк).

Задание 1. В современном русском языке можно усмотреть некоторую тенденцию, в соответствии с которой в одних случаях употребляется конструкция А, а в других – конструкция Б. Объясните, в чём состоит эта тенденция. Все ли примеры, приведённые выше, ей соответствуют? Если нет, с чем, по Вашему мнению, это может быть связано?

Задание 2. Раскройте скобки, использовав либо конструкцию А, либо конструкцию Б. Если в каких-то случаях выбор конструкции вызывает у Вас сомнения, отметьте это:

А. *Как водится, параллельно* ***(бумажная война)*** *происходила чехарда с собраниями акционеров* («Вечерняя Москва»)

Б. *Здесь, на советской территории, у самой границы и параллельно* ***(она)*** *проходит Августовский канал* (В. Суворов)

В. *Комната Франца выходила на улицу, шедшую параллельно* ***(набережная)*** (В. Набоков)

Г. *Они [фабрично-заводские комитеты] существовали параллельно* ***(профсоюзы)*** *и объединились с ними в 1918 г.* (Большая советская энциклопедия)

Д. *Скажем, в шекспировском «Короле Лире» сюжетная линия Лира развивается параллельно* ***(линия Глостера)*** (Т. Шабалина).

Задание 3. В последнее время в публицистике слово *параллельно* стало иногда употребляться ещё в одной конструкции – с предлогом *от*:

Е. *Религия должна существовать* ***параллельно от*** *гражданского общества.*

Ж. *Эта сторона жизни существовала где-то* ***параллельно от*** *меня и меня не затрагивала.*

З. *Наше государство всё ещё живёт* ***параллельно от*** *своих граждан.*

Попробуйте объяснить причины возникновения такой конструкции.

English translation:

The Russian word *parallel'no* 'in parallel' can govern nouns in dative case ('parallel to', construction A) as well as in instrumental case ('parallel with', construction B). Consider examples for both constructions.

1. *Vasich saw a small hollow. It was going* ***in parallel to*** *the Germans, blocking their way to the squadron* (G. Baklanov, 1961).
2. *Her way was to be* ***in parallel to*** *the tram route* (B. Pasternak, 1945–55).
3. *I did not like it that some people were climbing the hill* ***in parallel with*** *us, on both our sides* (F. Iskander, 1990).

4. *Now they were going* ***in parallel to*** *the embankment* (A. and B. Strugatsky, 1971).
5. *Winding up miles onto the cardan, I am driving* ***in parallel to*** *the wires* (V. Vyssotsky, 1971).
6. *A short summer tour in Riga was planned before the vacation,* ***in parallel with*** *the operation of the two theater stages in Moscow* (S. Pilyavskaya, 2001)
7. *New eight to nine-storey houses were standing in a broken line,* ***in parallel to*** *the boulevard* (Yu. Daniel, 1962).
8. *His much grown whisker was no longer sticking out* ***in parallel to*** *the ground surface, but was almost perpendicular to it, as if he was an old cat* (I. Il'f, E. Petrov, 1927–8).
9. *We were looking at some gazebos and churches above, enjoying a long cedar-tree alley, which went* ***in parallel with*** *the shore* (I. Goncharov, 1855–7).
10. *Finishing the façade is progressing* ***in parallel with*** *the mounting* («Komsomol'skaya Pravda» newspaper, 2007).
11. *Each year, the plant laborers find their life to be harder and harder, and the well-being of the managers, lawyers and a whole bunch of employees grows* ***in parallel with*** *it.* (D. Mamin-Sibiryak, 1874–5).

1. There is a tendency in modern Russian to use construction A and construction B in different cases. What is the difference? Does every example above comply with this tendency? If not, what could be the reason?

2. Choose either Construction A or Construction B for the following examples. In case you have difficulty with some sentences, explain why.

A. *As usual, a cockalorum with share holders meetings was happening in parallel to / with the paperwork war* («Evening Moscow» newspaper, 2007).

B. *Here, on Soviet territory, near the very border and in parallel to / with it, lies the Augustów Canal* (V. Suvorov, 1968–81).

C. *Franz's room had window to the street which was going in parallel to / with the quay* (V. Nabokov, 1927–8).

D. *They [factory and plant committees] existed in parallel to / with the trade unions and joined them in 1918* (Great Soviet Encyclopedia, 1969–78).

E. *Say, in King Lear by Shakespeare, the plot line of Lear is developing in parallel to / with the line of Gloucester* (T. Shabalina, early 2000s).

3. Lately, the Russian word *parallel'no* has been used in another construction, governing nouns in the genitive case:

F. *The religion should stay* ***in parallel from*** *the civil society.*

G. *This side of life was somewhere* ***in parallel from*** *myself and did not touch me.*

H. *Our state still lives* ***in parallel from*** *its citizens.*

Explain the reasons why this construction is emerging.

Solution of Problem # 3

Construction A (*in parallel to*) is used when referring to the spatial situation (e.g. of two lines being parallel to each other). Construction B (*in parallel with*) is used when referring to the temporal coincidence (e.g. of two simultaneous events). This can be explained by the inheritance of the government pattern from its cohyponyms or synonyms (*perpendikuljarno chemu-libo* 'perpendicular, vertical to smth' vs. *odnovremenno s chem-libo* 'simultaneously with smth'). One example does not comply with this rule, and it is the oldest one which dates back to the mid-19th century. Apparently, the rule is rather new (indeed, searching the corpus shows more counterexamples in the old texts; this can be shown when discussing the problem with the students and talking about corpus annotation). Construction C (*in parallel from*) is much newer, it can only be found in 21st century texts; this type of government is inherited from *nezavisimo* (*avtonomno*, *svobodno*) *ot chego-libo* 'independently from smth'.

Comment

This problem illustrates diachronic variation in Russian. It would be impossible to compose such a problem without using a corpus with rich metadata. Most of the examples come from the Russian National Corpus (http://www.ruscorpora.ru), but it turned out there are not enough examples of these constructions in the RNC. For this reason, some more examples had to be taken from the Internet. This illustrates the concept of Web as corpus (see also problem #6).

This problem was assigned at the Russian Linguistics Olympiad in 2007, and it did not include the dates of the texts. The high school students had to understand themselves that the excerpt from Ivan Goncharov's text is the oldest one. It was possible because Goncharov's novels are part of the school curriculum in Russia, and students can be expected to know when he lived. This shows that corpus-based problems sometimes require extralinguistic knowledge to account for the variation. Of course, the author of the problem has to be sure that all the solvers are expected to have such knowledge. This makes such problems similar to real-life linguistic research where one can never be confident whether all the information required for explaining the phenomenon is at hand.

Problem #4 (composed by Aleksandrs Berdicevskis)

Consider a Google Books Ngrams frequency diagram for three spellings of the same Russian word throughout the 20th century («Богъ», «Бог», «бог» 'God'). Which line corresponds to which spelling?

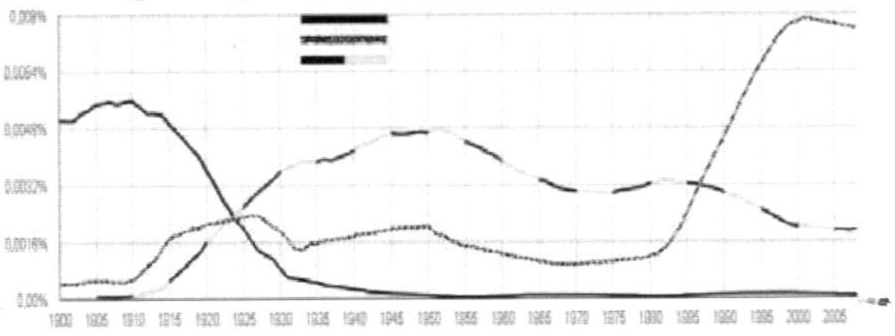

Solution of Problem # 4

The sharp frequency changes are caused by historical events which influenced Russian orthography: (1) the October revolution (and the orthography reform of 1918) and (2) the fall of the Soviet Union. Shortly before the revolution, the black line starts subsiding, while the gray line and the dotted line go up. After the revolution, the black line disappears, and the dotted line grows higher than the gray one and stays there until the fall of the Soviet Union. Therefore, the black line is the spelling *Богъ*, ending with the Ъ letter abolished after the Revolution. The dotted line is the spelling *бог*: during the Soviet rule, this word was never capitalized. The gray line stands for *Бог*, which is the present-day norm for the monotheistic deity. The dotted line, however, does not disappear, since the word for 'god' does not always reference such a deity.

Comment

This problem also presents a case of variation, namely diachronically motivated orthographic variation. This problem requires quite a lot of extralinguistic knowledge, but Russian high school students are expected to know about the history of the letter Ъ and the antireligious policy in the Soviet Union. The most important part of the problem is to connect this knowledge with the data represented on the graph.

3.3 Corpus examples illustrating synchronic variation and requiring statistical thinking

Problem #5 (composed by Alexander Piperski)

Russian hypocoristics (diminutive forms of personal names) are most often formed using two classes of suffixes: *-očk-/-ečk-* and *-on'k-/-en'k-*. Below are some names and the hypocoristics with these suffixes derived from them. Each hypocoristic is supplied with the number of texts in the Russian National Corpus (http://www.ruscorpora.ru) in which it occurs:

Base form	***-očk-/-ečk-***	***-on'k-/-en'k-***
Alla	*Alločka* – 48	*Allon'ka* – 1
An'a	*Anečka* – 111	*Anen'ka* – 2
Val'a	*Valečka* – 58	*Valen'ka* – 8
Vas'a	*Vasečka* – 9	*Vasen'ka* – 119
Volod'a	*Volodečka* – 15	*Voloden'ka* – 38
Glaša	*Glašečka* – 0	*Glašen'ka* – 11
Dima	*Dimočka* – 22	*Dimon'ka* – 0
Klava	*Klavočka* – 20	*Klavon'ka* – 0
Kol'a	*Kolečka* – 19	*Kolen'ka* – 73
Nad'a	*Nadečka* – 3	*Naden'ka* – 102
Pet'a	*Petečka* – 11	*Peten'ka* – 70
Saša	*Sašečka* – 4	*Sašen'ka* – 155
Sveta	*Svetočka* – 39	*Sveton'ka* – 0
Sen'a	*Senečka* – 15	*Senen'ka* – 0
Serëža	*Serëžečka* – 6	*Serëžen'ka* – 76
Tan'a	*Tanečka* – 120	*Tanen'ka* – 0
Tol'a	*Tolečka* – 17	*Tolen'ka* – 7
Jul'a	*Julečka* – 22	*Julen'ka* – 27

1. Here are six more pairs of hypocoristics:
Vitečka ~ Viten'ka
Olečka ~ Olen'ka
Lidočka ~ Lidon'ka
Sonečka ~ Sonen'ka
L'ubočka ~ L'ubon'ka
Jašečka ~ Jašen'ka

Try to predict for each of these pairs which hypocoristic occurs in more texts in the Russian National Corpus. If you cannot do that for some names, explain why.

Solution of problem #5

The choice of the suffix depends on the last consonant of the stem. *-očk-/-ečk-* is more frequent after non-palatalized ("hard") consonants and after *n'* (dissimilation). *-on'k-/-en'k-* is more frequent after hushing sibilants (*š*, *ž*; dissimilation) and after palatalized ("soft") consonants other than *n'*. For *l'* no rule can be stated.

Therefore, the expected more frequent forms are *Viten'ka*, *Lidočka*, *Lúbočka*, *Sonečka* and *Jašen'ka*. For *Olečka* ~ *Olen'ka* no prediction can be made.

Comment

This problem requires the ability to neglect introspection, since all Russian-speaking solvers have some intuitive judgements on the topic. It also shows that a linguist sometimes has to work with tendencies, rather than strict rules and leave some variation unexplained.

3.4 Other corpus-like data

Problem #6 (Composed by Vitaly Pavlenko)

In Turkish, the word *kadın* 'woman' is used when naming women by their profession, occupation, etc. This word can be placed before the noun referring to a profession as well as after it; there are no absolutely precise rules explaining it, but there is a certain tendency, according to which one of the two possible variants is used more often than the other.

Given are some Turkish phrases with the word *kadın* and their English translations. For the first 9 phrases, it is stated how many times they occur on the Internet as *kadın X* and how many times as *X kadın*. For the last 6 phrases the corresponding numbers are given to choose from:

Turkish phrase	translation
kadın barmen (40) *barmen kadın (191)*	barwoman
kadın dikişçi (2) *dikişçi kadın (112)*	seamstress
kadın hakem (1,910) *hakem kadın (107)*	female judge
kadın kasiyer (82) *kasiyer kadın (112)*	female cashier
kadın mühendis (3,350) *mühendis kadın (428)*	female engineer
kadın öğretmen (36,200) *öğretmen kadın (6,500)*	female teacher
kadın polis (41,200) *polis kadın (13,700)*	policewoman
kadın gazeteci (23,200) *gazeteci kadın (1,720)*	female journalist
kadın satıcı (400) *satıcı kadın (2,190)*	saleswoman
kadın avukat (...) *avukat kadın (...) 780 / 9,520*	female lawyer
kadın çevirmen (...) *çevirmen kadın (...) 29 / 1,630*	female translator
kadın fırıncı (...) *fırıncı kadın (...)10 / 275*	female baker
kadın ressam (...) *ressam kadın (...) 407 / 15,000*	female artist
kadın sütçü (...) *sütçü kadın (...) 97 / 758*	milkwoman
kadın terzi (...) *terzi kadın (...) 639 / 1,450*	tailoress

1. Put the right numbers into the brackets. Explain your reasoning.

Note. *ğ, ç, ş, ı, ö, ü* are special sounds of Turkish. The numbers given in the problem are Google hit counts as of October 23, 2008.

Solution of Problem #6

When used with the names of skilled occupations *kadın* is put before the noun, and with the names of service sector occupations *kadın* is put after the noun. The answer is as follows:

kadın avukat (9,520) *avukat kadın (780)*	female lawyer
kadın çevirmen (1,630) *çevirmen kadın (29)*	female translator
kadın fırıncı (10) *fırıncı kadın (275)*	female baker
kadın ressam (15,000) *ressam kadın (407)*	female artist
kadın sütçü (97) *sütçü kadın (758)*	milkwoman
kadın terzi (639) *terzi kadın (1,450)*	tailoress

Comment

As well as #5, this problem shows that linguists sometimes have to deal not with precise rules (as it is usually the case in traditional linguistics problems), but only with tendencies. It also demonstrates that search engines can be used in linguistic studies as large corpora. In this problem the exact difference between the two numbers does not matter (e.g., 82 vs. 112 is the same as 2 vs. 112 for the purposes of the problem), but similar problems might be created where the distance between the two numbers is essential.

4 Corpus linguistics problems: Some pitfalls

We have shown that corpus-based problems have some advantages over traditional types of problems. However, some of these can be regarded as weak sides, too.

Corpus linguistics problems illustrate linguistic phenomena with real data. Unfortunately, many sentences present in the corpus are rather large and sometimes even clumsy. If long sentences are used to illustrate the usage of just one word, there will inevitably be a lot of irrelevant information (cf. #1, #2, #3; each of the long sentences is intended to illustrate the behavior of a single word). On the other hand, the solvers might enjoy reading long real-life sentences instead of artificial examples.

Another issue that makes composing and using corpus-based problems difficult is the philosophy underlying such problems. In a typical problem that contains artificial data all phenomena must be explained by the solver. There is no place for unexplained variation. However, problems on corpus linguistics require statistical manner of thinking, rather than strictly deterministic conclusions. For example, problem #5 illustrates tendencies, some of which are more solid than the others. However, less frequent names do exist, which might baffle a solver who is used to explaining everything within a linguistics problem. In problem #4, the word *Богъ* which uses the old spelling did not vanish completely after the spelling reform of 1918. There is some noise at the bottom of the graph, and the solver has to understand that it is not necessary to account for this noise in order to solve the problem.

The authors of problems on corpus linguistics should also be aware that the methodology they demonstrate is not always sound. For instance, in problem #6 Google hit counts are used in spite of the fact that is has been shown many times that they cannot be trusted (cf. Kilgarriff 2007). Ideally, a problem on computational linguistics should be accompanied by an afterword explaining the drawbacks of the methods it uses. Otherwise it might be tempting for students to get a simplistic notion of corpus linguistics and its methodology.

5 Conclusion

The corpus is a valuable data source not only for linguistic studies, but also for composing linguistic problems. Corpus linguistics problems are useful to introduce the study of variation and the basics of statistical thinking in linguistics. However, they also have certain drawbacks, namely their length and unexplained variation within the data (which can however sometimes be an advantage bringing the problem closer to the real life). The main advantage of corpus-based problems is that real data are used, which can be verified and even more thoroughly studied by the student. Moreover, through such problems the students become acquainted with corpus linguistics as a research field that is rapidly gaining importance.

Acknowledgements

This research has been partially financed by a research program of History and Philology Branch of the Russian Academy of Sciences, a grant from the Russian Humanitarian Scientific Foundation No. 13-04-00307a, a President Grant for Leading Scientific Schools of Russia (No. NSh-6577.2012.6) and the Program of Strategic Development of the Russian State University for the Humanities. We would like to thank Aleksandrs Berdicevskis, Leonid Iomdin and Maria Konoshenko for valuable comments.

References

Adam Kilgarriff. 2007. Googleology is Bad Science. *Computational Linguistics* 33 (1): 147–51.

Boris L. Iomdin and Leonid L. Iomdin. 2011. Valency ambiguity interpretation: what can and what cannot be done. In: Proceedings of the 5th International Conference on Meaning-Text Theory. Barcelona, September 8–9, 2011. Ed. by Igor Boguslavsky and Leo Wanner. Barcelona: University Pompeu-Fabra.

Ivan A. Derzhanski, Aleksandr S. Berdichevskij, Ksenia A. Guiliarova, Boris L. Iomdin, Elena V. Muravenko, and Maria L. Rubinstein. 2004. O perevodimosti lingvisticheskix zadach: Uroki pervoj mezhdunarodnoj lingvisticheskoj olimpiady [On translatability of linguistic problems: Lessons of the First International Linguistics Olympiad]. In: *Computational linguistics and intellectual technologies*. Papers from the annual international conference "Dialogue". Moscow: Nauka, pp. 240–5.

Introducing Computational Concepts in a Linguistics Olympiad

Patrick Littell
Department of Linguistics
University of British Columbia
Vancouver, BC V6T1Z4, Canada
littell@interchange.ubc.ca

Lori Levin
Language Technologies Institute
Carnegie Mellon University
Pittsburgh, PA 15213, USA
lsl@cs.cmu.edu

Jason Eisner
Computer Science Department
Johns Hopkins University
Baltimore, MD 21218, USA
jason@cs.jhu.edu

Dragomir R. Radev
Department of EECS
School of Information
and Department of Linguistics
University of Michigan
radev@umich.edu

Abstract

Linguistics olympiads, now offered in more than 20 countries, provide secondary-school students a compelling introduction to an unfamiliar field. The North American Computational Linguistics Olympiad (NACLO) includes computational puzzles in addition to purely linguistic ones. This paper explores the computational subject matter we seek to convey via NACLO, as well as some of the challenges that arise when adapting problems in computational linguistics to an audience that may have no background in computer science, linguistics, or advanced mathematics. We present a small library of reusable design patterns that have proven useful when composing puzzles appropriate for secondary-school students.

1 What is a Linguistics Olympiad?

A linguistics olympiad (LO) (Payne and Derzhanski, 2010) is a puzzle contest for secondary-school students in which contestants compete to solve self-contained linguistics problem sets. LOs have their origin in the Moscow Traditional Olympiad in Linguistics, established in 1965, and have since spread around the world; an international contest (http://www.ioling.org) has been held yearly since 2003.

In an LO, every problem set is self-contained, so no prior experience in linguistics is necessary to compete. In fact, LO contests are fun and rewarding for exactly this reason: by the end of the contest, contestants are managing to read hieroglyphics, conjugate verbs in Swahili, and perform other amazing feats. Furthermore, they have accomplished this solely through their own analytical abilities and linguistic intuition.

Based on our experience going into high schools and presenting our material, this "linguistic" way of thinking about languages almost always comes as a novel surprise to students. They largely think about languages as collections of known facts that you learn in classes and from books, not something that you can dive into and figure out for yourself. This is a hands-on antidote to the common public misconception that linguists are fundamentally polyglots, rather than language scientists, and students come out of the experience having realized that linguistics is a very different field (and hopefully a more compelling one) than they had assumed it to be.

2 Computational Linguistics at the LO

Our goal, since starting the North American Computational Linguistics Olympiad (NACLO) in 2007 (Radev et al., 2008), has been to explore how this LO experience can be used to introduce students to computational linguistics. Topics in computational linguistics have been featured before in LOs, occasionally in the Moscow LO and with some regularity in the Bulgarian LO.

Our deliberations began with some troubling statistics regarding enrollments in computer science programs (Zweben, 2013). Between 2003 and 2007 enrollments in computer science dropped dramatically. This was attributed in part to the dip in the IT sector, but it also stemmed in part from a perception problem in which teenagers view computer science careers as mundane and boring: "I don't want to be Dilbert,[1] sitting in a cubicle programming payroll software my whole life." This is an unrealistically narrow perception of the kinds of problems computer scientists tackle, and NACLO began in part as a way to publicize to teenagers that many interesting problems can be approached using computational methods.

Although enrollments are not yet back to the 2003 levels, there has been a sharp increase since 2007 (Zweben, 2013). The resurgence can be attributed in part to the strength of the IT sector, but also to the realization that computer science is relevant to almost every area of science and technology (Thibodeau, 2013). NACLO aims to be part of this trend by showing students that computer science is used in studying fascinating problems related to human language.

Even "traditional" LO puzzles are inherently computational in that they require pattern recognition, abstraction, generalization, and establishing and pruning a solution space. However, we also want to teach computational linguistics more explicitly. NACLO puzzles have featured a wide variety of topics in computational linguistics and computer science; they may focus on the application itself, or on concepts, tools, and algorithms that underlie the applications. Broadly, computational LO topics fall into three types, summarized below.

2.1 Technological applications

NACLO has included puzzles on technologies that most people are familiar with, including spell checking, information retrieval, machine translation, document summarization, and dialogue systems. In a typical applications puzzle, the contestants would discover how the application works, how it handles difficult cases, or what its limitations are. In "Summer Eyes" (Radev and Hesterberg, 2009), the contestant discovers the features that are used for selecting sentences in a summarization program, including the position of a sentence in the article, the number of words the sentence shares with the title, etc. In "Springing Up Baby" (Srivastava and Bender, 2008) and "Running on MT" (Somers, 2011), contestants explore word sense disambiguation in the context of machine translation, while "Tiger Tale" (Radev, 2011) highlights some realistic sources of knowledge for machine translation such as cognates and cross-language syntactic similarities. "Thorny Stems" (Breck, 2008) and "A fox among the h" (Littell, 2012b) introduce stemming.

2.2 Formal grammars and algorithms

Some puzzles introduce the formal tools of computational linguistics and linguistic concepts that are important in computational linguistics, often in a whimsical way. For example, "Sk8 Parsr" (Littell, 2009) introduces shift-reduce parsing by means of a hypothetical skateboarding video game. "Aw-TOM-uh-tuh" (Littell, 2008) introduces a finite-state machine that determines which strings form legal words in the Rotokas language. "Orwellspeak" (Eisner, 2009) asks solvers to modify a simple context-free grammar, and then to discover that a 4-gram model cannot model this language without precision or recall errors. "Twodee" (Eisner, 2012) invents a two-dimensional writing system, shown below, as a vehicle for helping students discover parsing ambiguity—and production ambiguity—without the full formal apparatus of grammars, nonterminals, or tree notation.

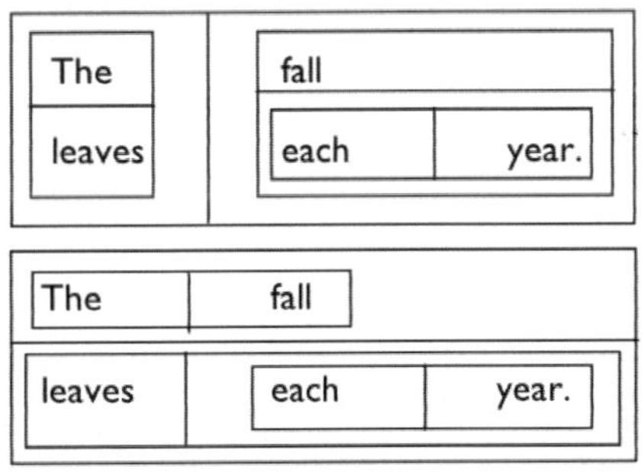

"The Little Engine That Could... Read" (Littell and Pustejovsky, 2012) explores quantifier monotonicity, while "Grice's Grifter Gadgets" (Boyd-Graber, 2013) covers Grice's maxims as part of the specification of a computerized game assistant.

2.3 Computational concepts

NACLO puzzles have also introduced computational concepts that go beyond computational linguistics. "Texting, Texting, One Two Three" (Littell, 2010b) and "The Heads and Tails of Huffman" (DeNero, 2013) introduce data compression. "One, Two, Tree" (Smith et al., 2012) introduces the Catalan numbers and other recurrences via binary bracketing of ambiguous compound nouns.

[1]An engineer in the eponymous American comic strip, Dilbert has a famously dysfunctional workplace and unrewarding job.

"Nok-nok" (Fink, 2009) introduces Levenshtein distance by describing a hypothetical typing tutor for very bad spellers.

3 The Challenge of Writing Computational Problems

To achieve our goals, it becomes necessary to write computational linguistics puzzles in such a way that they are self-contained, requiring no prior experience in linguistics, computer science, or advanced math. This has proven very difficult, but not impossible, and in the past seven years we have managed to learn a lot about how to (and how not to) write them.

Perhaps the hardest part of writing any LO puzzle is that authors have to remove themselves from their knowledge and experience: to forget technical definitions of "phrase" or "noun" or "string" or "function," and to forget the facts and insights and history that formed our modern understanding of these. This is doubly hard when it comes to puzzles involving computational methods. The ability to write an algorithm that a computer could actually interpret is a specialized skill that we learned through education, and it is very, very hard to back up and imagine what it would be like to not be able to think like this. (It is almost like trying to remember what it was like to not be able to read—not simply not knowing a particular alphabet or language, but not even understanding how reading would work.)

Here is an illustration of an interesting but nonetheless inappropriate LO puzzle:

> *Here are fourteen English compound words:*
>
> | | |
> |---|---|
> | birdhouse | housework |
> | blackbird | tablespoon |
> | blackboard | teacup |
> | boardroom | teaspoon |
> | boathouse | workhouse |
> | cupboard | workroom |
> | houseboat | worktable |
>
> *Even if you didn't know any English, you could probably determine by looking at this list which English words were used to make up the compounds: "black", "bird", "board", etc...*
>
> *How would you do this if you were a computer?*

This task, although potentially appropriate for a programming competition, is inappropriate for an LO: the intended task requires some prior knowledge about what computers can and cannot do. Note that nowhere in the puzzle itself are the properties of this imaginary computer specified. It is assumed that the solver knows roughly the state of modern computing machinery and what kinds of instructions it can execute.

Imagine for a moment what a right answer to this puzzle would look like, and then picture what a wrong answer might look like. Your right answer was probably an algorithm that could run on an abstract computer with capabilities very much like real computers. The wrong answer probably made incorrect assumptions about what sorts of operations computers are capable of, or treated enormously complex operations as if they were primitive.[2]

The problem with the above puzzle is that it is very open-ended, and in the absence of a large body of shared knowledge between the author and the solver, the solver cannot know what it is the author wants or when they have solved it to the author's satisfaction.

In order to avoid this, it is best to set up the puzzle so that the "search space" for possible answers is relatively constrained, and the "win" conditions are clear. Ideally, if a contestant has solved a puzzle, they should know they have solved it, and thus be able to move on confidently to the next puzzle.[3] In this respect, LO puzzles are akin to crossword puzzles, problems from other Olympiads, or online puzzle games. This feeling of accomplishment is key to the kind of rewarding learning experience that have made LOs so successful.

4 Design Patterns for CL Puzzles

Over the years, we have found several reliable strategies for turning ideas and topics from computational linguistics into solvable, rewarding puz-

[2]Keep in mind that today's contestants were born in the late 1990s. They are unlikely to even remember a world without ubiquitous Internet and powerful natural language search. Their conception of "what computers basically do" is not necessarily going to be the same as those of us who encountered computers when they were still recognizable as a kind of sophisticated calculator.

[3]This is not to say, however, that only those who solve a puzzle in its entirety should feel accomplished or rewarded. The best puzzles often contain layers of mysteries: it may be that only a few will solve every mystery in the puzzle, but most contestants come away with the satisfaction of having discovered something.

zles.

Not every computational puzzle makes use of these—some are entirely unique—but many do. In addition, these strategies are not mutually exclusive; many computational puzzles utilize several of these at once. For example, a "Broken Machine" puzzle may then present the solver with a "Troublemaker" task, or an "Assembly Required" machine may, upon assembly, turn out to be a "Broken" one.

4.1 Assembly Required

The solver is presented with a task to complete, and also a partially specified algorithm for doing so. The partial specification illustrates the desired formal notation and the model of computation. But it may be missing elements, or the ordering or relationship between the elements is unclear, or some other aspect of the system remains unfinished. The solver is asked to complete the system so that it performs the appropriate task or produces the appropriate outputs.

For example, NACLO 2008 included a puzzle on stemming, "Thorny Stems" (Breck, 2008), in which contestants help develop an algorithm to isolate the stems of various words. In this puzzle, the solver is not required to invent an algorithm *ex nihilo*; this would merely have rewarded those who already understand algorithms, not introduce algorithmic thinking to neophytes. Instead, the overall structure of the intended algorithm (an ordered sequence of if-thens) is made explicit, and the solver's task is to fill in the details:

> Rule 1: If a word ends in _____, then replace _____ with _____ to form the stem.
>
> Rule 2: If a word ends in _____, then replace _____ with _____ to form the stem.

In another puzzle from the same contest, "Aw-TOM-uh-tuh" (Littell, 2008), the solver must complete an unfinished finite-state automaton so that it performs a language recognition task. The solver is given a brief introduction to FSAs and a simple sample FSA, and then given an incomplete FSA whose labels lack edges. The solver's task is to place the labels on the correct edges so that the FSA accepts certain inputs and rejects others.

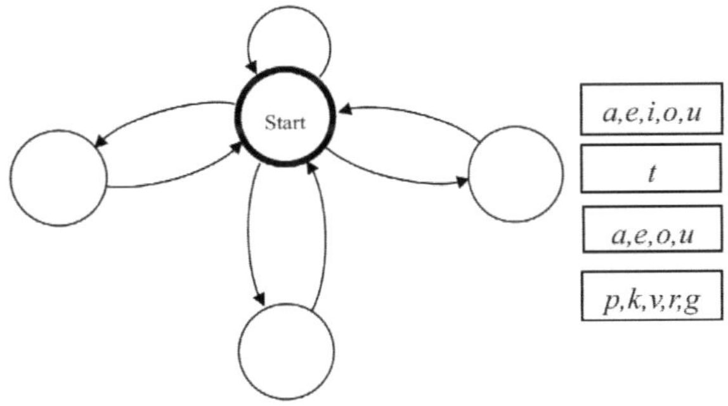

Other examples of the "Assembly Required" pattern can be found in the puzzles "Sk8 Parsr" (Littell, 2009), "The Heads and Tails of Huffman" (DeNero, 2013), and "BrokEnglish!" (Littell, 2011).

4.2 Black Box

The solver is presented with the inputs to a system and the outputs, and must work out how the system generated the outputs. Unlike in the "Assembly Required" pattern, little or no information about the algorithm is provided to the solver; the solver's fundamental task is to characterize this unknown algorithm as thoroughly as possible.

For example, NACLO 2010 featured a puzzle on Huffman text compression, "Texting, Texting, One Two Three" (Littell, 2010b), in which an unspecified algorithm converts strings of letters to strings of numbers:

> Testing testing = 33222143224142341-1222143224142341331
>
> Does anyone copy = 33233322143131-42343324221124232342343331

Working out the basic number-letter correspondences is relatively straightforward, but the real puzzle is working out the rationale behind these correspondences. Some of the answers require letters (like "r" and "x") that do not occur anywhere in the data, but can be deduced once the system as a whole is fully understood.

NACLO 2009 featured a puzzle on Levenshtein distance, "Nok-nok!" (Fink, 2009), that also used this pattern. In it, a spell-checker is rating how well (or poorly) a user has spelled a word.

User Input	Correct word	Output
owll	owl	"almost right"
ples	please	"quite close"
reqird	required	"quite close"
plez	please	"a bit confusing"
mispeln	misspelling	"very confusing"

The solver's task is to work out the algorithm sufficiently to predict how the system would respond to novel inputs.

Other examples of the "Black Box" pattern can be found in "The Deschamps Codice" (Piperski, 2012) and "The Little Engine that Could... Read" (Littell and Pustejovsky, 2012).

Depending on the intended algorithm, the "Black Box" pattern may or may not be appropriate. This pattern works best when the nature of the transformation between input and output is relatively straightforward and the purpose of the transformation is relatively clear. In the Huffman coding puzzle, for example, the nature of the transformation is entirely obvious (replace letters with number sequences) and thus the solution space of the puzzle is relatively constrained (figure out which letters correspond to which number sequences and then try to figure out why). In the spell-checking puzzle, the purpose of the transformation is easily understood, giving the solver a head start on figuring out which features of the input the algorithm might be considering.

When the nature of the transformation is less obvious—for example, the generation of numbers of unclear significance, rating some unknown aspect of a text passage—"Black Box" is not as appropriate as the other patterns. The potential problem is that not only must the solver come up with an algorithm on their own, they must come up with the same algorithm the author did. Given a complicated algorithm, even small implementation details may lead to very different outputs, so a solver can even have found a basically correct solution but nevertheless not managed to produce the intended outputs.

In such cases, the "Assembly Required" or "Broken Machine" patterns are potentially more appropriate.

4.3 Broken Machine

The solver is presented with a system that purports to perform a particular task, but actually fails on particular inputs. The solver is tasked with figuring out what went wrong and, potentially, fixing the system so that it works. In some cases, the system simply has an error in it; in others, the system is correct but cannot handle certain difficult cases.

NACLO has featured a wide variety of broken machines, often with humorous outputs. "Help my Camera!" (Bender, 2009) features a dialogue system that could not correctly resolve pronoun references:

> Human: "There's this restaurant on Bancroft that's supposed to be really good that I heard about from my mother. Can you help me find it?"
> Computer: "Where did you last see your mother?"

"BrokEnglish!" (Littell, 2011) features a runaway script that replaced certain ISO 639-1 codes with language names:

> Hebrewy, ChamorRomanianrICHebrewcHebrewnlandic! whEnglish you get a FrEnglishcHebrewe momEnglisht, cHebrewck out thICHebrewcHebrewnlandic niCHebrewcHebrewn little pRomaniangram i wRomaniante.

Solvers are then tasked with determining why this script produced such a bizarre output, and additionally tasked with determining in what order the replacements had to have occurred in order to get this exact output.

"Orwellspeak" (Eisner, 2009) involves a context-free grammar that produces sentences that were grammatically correct but counter to the ideals of a fictional totalitarian Party. The solver must rewrite the grammar so that only "correct" thoughts can be uttered. In the second part of the puzzle, the solver must show that Markov models would be *inherently* broken.

Other examples of "Broken Machines" are "The Lost Tram" (Iomdin, 2007), "Sk8 Parsr" (Littell, 2009), "A fox among the h" (Littell, 2012b), "The Little Engine that Could... Read" (Littell and Pustejovsky, 2012), and "Grice's Grifter Gadgets" (Boyd-Graber, 2013).

4.4 Troublemaker

The solver is presented with a system and some sample inputs and outputs, and must discover an input that causes the system to fail, or produce outputs that are strange, suboptimal, or have some unusual property.

Few puzzles make use of only the "Troublemaker" pattern. Many are basically "Assembly Required" or "Broken Machine" puzzles that use a "Troublemaker" task to get the contestant thinking about the ways in which the system is limited or imperfect. They are also often creative—the contestant usually invents their own inputs—and thus can serve as a refreshing change of pace.[4]

NACLO 2009 featured a "Broken Machine" puzzle about shift-reduce parsing ("Sk8 Parsr") (Littell, 2009), couched in terms of a fictional skateboarding videogame. The solver is given an algorithm by which button presses are transformed into skateboard trick "combos" like those shown below, but many well-formed "combos" cannot correctly be parsed due to a shift-reduce conflict.

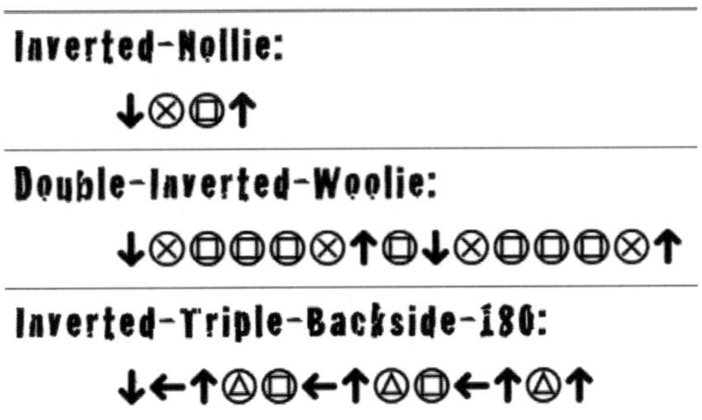

The solver is given an example of one such class of inputs, and then asked to discover other classes of inputs that likewise fail.

"Troublemaker" puzzles are not always couched in terms of bugs. "This problem is pretty // easy" (Radev, 2007a) asks solvers to construct eye-catching garden path sentences. In the Huffman text compression puzzle detailed above ("Texting, Texting, One Two Three") (Littell, 2010b), a "Troublemaker" task is introduced to get contestants thinking about the limits of compression. Although the compression algorithm is not "broken" in any way, any compression algorithm will "fail" on some possible input and return an output longer than the input, and the solver is tasked to discover such an input.

"Troublemaker" tasks can also be found in "Grammar Rules" (Schalley and Littell, 2013) and "Yesbot" (Mitkov and Littell, 2013).

[4]If the "Troublemaker" task asks for an input with a particular formal property (i.e., a sentence generated or not generated from a particular grammar), automated grading scripts can determine the correctness of the answer without human intervention. This means that contestants can get a chance to enter "creative" answers even in large contests (like the NACLO Open Round) that utilize automatic grading.

4.5 Jabberwock

Not all puzzle types revolve around abstract machines. Another recurring puzzle type, the "Jabberwock", involves asking the solver to puzzle out the syntactic or semantic properties of unknown words. Often these words are nonsense words, but this puzzle type can also work on natural language data. To perform this task, solvers often have to use the same methods that a computer would.

"We are all molistic in a way" (Radev, 2007b) asks solvers to infer the polarity of various nonsense adjectives based on a series of sentences.[5]

> The teacher is danty and cloovy.
> Mary is blitty but cloovy.
> Strungy and struffy, Diane was a pleasure to watch.
> Even though weasy, John is strungy.
> Carla is blitty but struffy.

The solver must work out from sentences such as these whether words like "danty" and "weasy" have positive or negative associations. In doing so, the solver has essentially constructed and solved a semi-supervised learning problem.

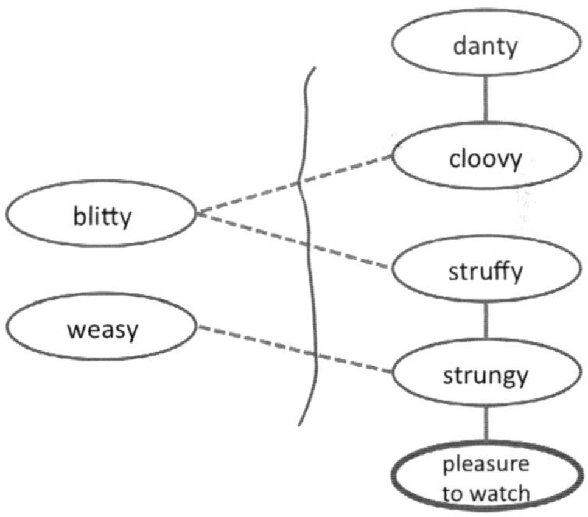

In "Gelda's House of Gelbelgarg" (Littell, 2010a), solvers are presented with a page of fabricated restaurant reviews for an entirely fictional cuisine:

> "A hidden gem in Lower Uptown! Get the färsel-försel with gorse-weebel and you'll have a happy stomach for a week. And top it off with a flebba of sweet-bolger while you're at it!"

[5]The list given here includes a subset of the examples used in the real puzzle in 2007.

> "I found the food confusing and disorienting. Where is this from? I randomly ordered the färsel-försel and had to send them back!"

Using various grammatical cues (article and pronoun choice, "less" vs. "fewer", etc.), solvers have to sort the items into things most likely to be discrete, countable objects, things most likely to be liquids or masses, and things most likely to be containers or measures.

This type of puzzle often violates the common LO restriction on using nonsense words and made-up languages, but it is not always possible to base this sort of puzzle on a completely unfamiliar language. Many "Jabberwock" puzzles involve inferring syntactic or semantic information about unknown words in an otherwise known language. The two puzzles above therefore require contestants to consult their own intuitions about English. These puzzles would have been entirely different (and prohibitively difficult) if the language had been completely unfamiliar.

Other Jabberwock puzzles include "Tiger Tale" (Radev, 2011) and "Cat and Mouse Story" (Littell, 2012a).

4.6 Combinatorial Problems

Some puzzles effectively force the solver to design *and* run an algorithm, to get an answer that would be too difficult to compute by brute force. Such puzzles involve computational thinking. But since the solver only has to give the *output* of the algorithm, there is no need to agree on a type of computing device or a notation for writing algorithms down.

Such puzzles include combinatorial tasks that involve the counting, maximization, or existence of linguistic objects. They require mathematical and algorithmic skills (just as in math or programming competitions), and demonstrate how these skills apply to linguistics or NLP.

Portions of "One, Two, Tree" (Smith et al., 2012) and "Twodee" (Eisner, 2012) require solvers to count all ways to parse a sentence, or to count all sentences of a certain type. Because the counts are large, the solver must find the pattern, which involves writing down a closed-form formula such as 2^n or a more complex dynamic programming recurrence.

5 Conclusions

Researchers and teachers from the ACL community are invited to contact the NACLO organizing committee at `naclo14org@umich.edu`[6] with their ideas for new puzzles or new types of puzzles. All of the past puzzles and solutions can be browsed at `http://www.naclo.cs.cmu.edu/practice.html`. In general, puzzles in Round 1 each year should be easier and automatically gradable. Puzzles in Round 2 permit more involved questions and answers; this is a smaller contest in which the top Round 1 scorers (usually, the top 10 percent) can qualify for the International Linguistic Olympiad.

Thus far, NACLO's computational puzzles have reached at least 6,000 students at more than 150 testing sites[7] in the U.S. and Canada, as well as at least 10,000 students in the three other English-language countries that share LO puzzles with NACLO.

We observe that most computational puzzles do not need obscure languages, staying on the contestant's home turf of English and technology. This does *not* mean, however, that the computational puzzles are purely formal and lack linguistic content. Some of them in fact probe subtle facts about English (the introspective method in linguistics), and some of them cover areas of linguistics that are underserved by traditional LO puzzles. Traditional LO puzzles instead ask the solver to sort out vocabulary and basic morphophonological or orthographic patterns in a mystery language (the fieldwork method in linguistics). Students who enjoy "top-down" thinking or who are deeply interested in "how to do things with words" may prefer the former kind of puzzle.

Competitions are popular in many North American high schools, perhaps in part as a way to impress college admissions officers. We have exploited this to give students a taste of our interdisciplinary field before they choose a college major. Some students may be specifically attracted to NACLO by the word "computational" or the word "linguistics," or may be intrigued by their juxtaposition. Many NACLO participants reveal that they had started to study linguistics on their own before encountering NACLO, and have welcomed

[6] Or `nacloXXorg@umich.edu`, where XX is the last two digits of the calendar year of the upcoming February.

[7] NACLO tests have been given at more than 100 high schools and more than 50 university sites; the latter are open to students from all local high schools.

NACLO as an outlet for their enthusiasm and a place where they can interact with other students who have the same interests.

NACLO's past puzzles remain freely available on the web for anyone who is interested. Two volumes of NACLO-style puzzles (most of them from real competitions), edited by program chair Dragomir Radev, have recently been published by Springer (Radev, 2013a; Radev, 2013b). Adult hobbyists and home-schooled students may discover computational linguistics through encountering these puzzles. Avid LO contestants use them to prepare for upcoming contests. Finally, high school and college teachers can use them as the basis of whole-class or small-group classroom activities that expose students to computational thinking.

Acknowledgments

We would like to thank the National Science Foundation for supporting NACLO through the following grants: IIS0633871, BCS1137828, and IIS0838848. We also express our gratitude to NSF program managers Tatiana Korelsky, Terry Langendoen, and Joan Maling for their effort in initiating and maintaining NACLO. The Linguistic Society of America and the North American Chapter of the Association for Computational Linguistics provide ongoing support. Other sponsors, volunteers, and problem writers are too numerous to name. They are listed on the contest booklets each year, which can be found on the NACLO web site: http://www.naclo.cs.cmu.edu.

References

Emily Bender. 2009. Help my camera! In *North American Computational Linguistics Olympiad 2009*. http://www.naclo.cs.cmu.edu/assets/problems/naclo09F.pdf.

Jordan Boyd-Graber. 2013. Grice's grifter gadgets. In *North American Computational Linguistics Olympiad 2013*. http://www.naclo.cs.cmu.edu/2013/NACLO2013ROUND2.pdf.

Eric Breck. 2008. Thorny stems. In *North American Computational Linguistics Olympiad 2008*. http://www.naclo.cs.cmu.edu/assets/problems/NACLO08h.pdf.

John DeNero. 2013. The heads and tails of Huffman. In *North American Computational Linguistics Olympiad 2013*. http://www.naclo.cs.cmu.edu/2013/NACLO2013ROUND1.pdf.

Jason Eisner. 2009. Orwellspeak. In *North American Computational Linguistics Olympiad 2009*. http://www.naclo.cs.cmu.edu/assets/problems/naclo09M.pdf.

Jason Eisner. 2012. Twodee. In *North American Computational Linguistics Olympiad 2013*. http://www.naclo.cs.cmu.edu/problems2012/NACLO2012ROUND2.pdf.

Eugene Fink. 2009. Nok-nok! In *North American Computational Linguistics Olympiad 2009*. http://www.naclo.cs.cmu.edu/assets/problems/naclo09B.pdf.

Boris Iomdin. 2007. The lost tram. In *North American Computational Linguistics Olympiad 2007*. http://www.naclo.cs.cmu.edu/assets/problems/naclo07_f.pdf.

Patrick Littell and James Pustejovsky. 2012. The little engine that could...read. In *North American Computational Linguistics Olympiad 2012*. http://www.naclo.cs.cmu.edu/problems2012/NACLO2012ROUND2.pdf.

Patrick Littell. 2008. Aw-TOM-uh-tuh. In *North American Computational Linguistics Olympiad 2008*. http://www.naclo.cs.cmu.edu/assets/problems/NACLO08i.pdf.

Patrick Littell. 2009. Sk8 parsr. In *North American Computational Linguistics Olympiad 2009*. http://www.naclo.cs.cmu.edu/assets/problems/naclo09G.pdf.

Patrick Littell. 2010a. Gelda's house of gelbelgarg. In *North American Computational Linguistics Olympiad 2010*. http://www.naclo.cs.cmu.edu/problems2010/A.pdf.

Patrick Littell. 2010b. Texting, texting, one two three. In *North American Computational Linguistics Olympiad 2010*. http://www.naclo.cs.cmu.edu/problems2010/E.pdf.

Patrick Littell. 2011. BrokEnglish! In *North American Computational Linguistics Olympiad 2011*. http://www.naclo.cs.cmu.edu/problems2011/E.pdf.

Patrick Littell. 2012a. Cat and mouse story. In *North American Computational Linguistics Olympiad 2012*. http://www.naclo.cs.cmu.edu/problems2012/NACLO2012ROUND1.pdf.

Patrick Littell. 2012b. A fox among the h. In *North American Computational Linguistics Olympiad 2012*. http://www.naclo.cs.cmu.edu/problems2012/NACLO2012ROUND2.pdf.

Ruslan Mitkov and Patrick Littell. 2013. Grammar rules. In *North American Computational Linguistics Olympiad 2013*. http://www.naclo.cs.cmu.edu/2013/NACLO2013ROUND2.pdf.

Thomas E. Payne and Ivan Derzhanski. 2010. The linguistics olympiads: Academic competitions in linguistics for secondary school students. In Kristin Denham and Anne Lobeck, editors, *Linguistics at school*. Cambridge University Press.

Alexander Piperski. 2012. The Deschamps codice. In *North American Computational Linguistics Olympiad 2012*. http://www.naclo.cs.cmu.edu/problems2012/NACLO2012ROUND2.pdf.

Dragomir Radev and Adam Hesterberg. 2009. Summer eyes. In *North American Computational Linguistics Olympiad 2009*. http://www.naclo.cs.cmu.edu/assets/problems/naclo09E.pdf.

Dragomir R. Radev, Lori Levin, and Thomas E. Payne. 2008. The North American Computational Linguistics Olympiad (NACLO). In *Proceedings of the Third Workshop on Issues in Teaching Computational Linguistics*, pages 87–96, Columbus, Ohio, June. Association for Computational Linguistics. http://www.aclweb.org/anthology/W/W08/W08-0211.

Dragomir Radev. 2007a. This problem is pretty // easy. In *North American Computational Linguistics Olympiad 2007*. http://www.naclo.cs.cmu.edu/assets/problems/naclo07_h.pdf.

Dragomir Radev. 2007b. We are all molistic in a way. In *North American Computational Linguistics Olympiad 2007*. http://www.naclo.cs.cmu.edu/assets/problems/naclo07_a.pdf.

Dragomir Radev. 2011. Tiger tale. In *North American Computational Linguistics Olympiad 2011*. http://www.naclo.cs.cmu.edu/problems2011/F.pdf.

Dragomir Radev, editor. 2013a. *Puzzles in Logic, Languages, and Computation: The Green Book*. Springer: Berlin.

Dragomir Radev, editor. 2013b. *Puzzles in Logic, Languages, and Computation: The Red Book*. Springer: Berlin.

Andrea Schalley and Patrick Littell. 2013. Grammar rules! In *North American Computational Linguistics Olympiad 2013*. http://www.naclo.cs.cmu.edu/2013/NACLO2013ROUND1.pdf.

Noah Smith, Kevin Gimpel, and Jason Eisner. 2012. One, two, tree. In *North American Computational Linguistics Olympiad 2012*. http://www.naclo.cs.cmu.edu/problems2012/NACLO2012ROUND2.pdf.

Harold Somers. 2011. Running on MT. In *North American Computational Linguistics Olympiad 2011*. http://www.naclo.cs.cmu.edu/problems2011/A.pdf.

Ankit Srivastava and Emily Bender. 2008. Springing up baby. In *North American Computational Linguistics Olympiad 2008*. http://www.naclo.cs.cmu.edu/assets/problems/prob08b.pdf.

Patrick Thibodeau. 2013. Computer science enrollments soared last year, rising 30%, March. http://www.computerworld.com/s/article/9237459/Computer_science_enrollments_soared_last_year_rising_30_.

Stuart Zweben. 2013. Computing degree and enrollment trends, March. http://cra.org/govaffairs/blog/wp-content/uploads/2013/03/CRA_Taulbee_CS_Degrees_and_Enrollment_2011-12.pdf.

Multilingual Editing of Linguistic Problems

Ivan Derzhanski
Department of Mathematical Linguistics
Institute of Mathematics and Informatics
Bulgarian Academy of Sciences
iad58g@gmail.com

Abstract

Multilinguality has been an essential feature of the International Linguistic Olympiad since its conception. Although deemed most desirable, the production of a problem set in several parallel versions and the verification of their equivalence is a time-consuming and error-prone task. This paper tells about the efforts to develop tools and methods which increase its efficiency and reliability.

1 Introduction

In September 2003 the 1st International Linguistics Olympiad (IOL, *née* International Olympiad in Theoretical, Mathematical and Applied Linguistics), an annual contest for secondary-school students in solving self-sufficient linguistic problems (Derzhanski, Payne 2009), took place in Bulgaria. Six countries were represented by a total of 33 participants. At the 10th instalment in 2012 the countries were 26, the contestants 131, and both numbers keep growing.

Since its launching, multilinguality has been a crucial feature of IOL. A linguistic problem depends more on the language in which it is formulated than a problem in, e.g., mathematics: not every problem can work in all languages, and even when it can, producing versions which give equal chances to all contestants is not always straightforward. For this reason at IOL, unlike many other international fora, there is no question of limiting the working languages to one or just a few. Accordingly their number has grown from five at IOL1 to fifteen at IOL10.[1] For the same reason the versions of the problem set in all working languages can't be created immediately before the contest, as is done at some of the other international science olympiads; they need to be prepared and verified well in advance.

The production of the multilingual package is a time-consuming and error-prone task, and it calls for the development of tools and methods to increase its efficiency and reliability.

2 The Past: IOL1

A linguistic problem is composed of language material and surrounding text; the language material in turn consists of data in unfamiliar languages and in Solverese[2] (usually translations of the unfamiliar language data). In a multilingual edition of the problem set it is imperative that the Solverese parts be equivalent and everything else be identical.

Figure 1 presents half a page from the Dutch and the English versions of the IOL1 problem set. It is easy to see that the formatting, the formulae and the Egyptian Arabic expressions had to be exactly the same.

In order to minimise the effort needed to edit the problems in all working languages and the chance that a technical mishap might create a divergence where none should occur, an *ad hoc* method was invented. The problem set was written in LaTeX, [3] with a master source file for each

[1] In fact at IOL1 and some subsequent early IOLs the versions that were made outnumbered the actual working languages by one, because an English version was made, although not used at the contest, for general reference and for advertising. At some of the recent IOLs, too, there have been more versions than working languages, as the versions in British and American English have been separate, though only differing in the format of the dates and in the spelling of a few words.

[2] On this term see (Bozhanov, Derzhanski 2013, fn. 2).

[3] This choice was made because TeX is not a mere typesetting system but a full-fledged programming environment, which enables some of the text to be computed rather than typed, greatly reducing the danger of typographic errors. The most powerful inspiration was (Knuth 1986, p. 218); see also (Derzhanski 2009, Appendix A).

1. ITO: Borovets '03. Individuele wedstrijd

Opgave 2 (25 punten)

Hieronder staan rekenkundige vergelijkingen in het Egyptische dialect van het Arabisch[1]. Alle onderdelen voor en na het "=" teken zijn breuken waarin de tellers en noemers niet hoger zijn dan 10. (Alleen het rechterdeel van de laatste som is hierop een uitzondering.) Er is ook geen noemer, die gelijk is aan 1:

tumn + *tumnēn* = *talatt itmān* (1)

sabaʕt itlāt + *suds* = *ʕašart irbāʕ* (2)

tusʕēn + *tusʕ* = *sudsēn* (3)

xamast ixmās + *subʕ* = *tamant isbāʕ* (4)

subʕēn + *xumsēn* = $\frac{24}{35}$ (5)

Opdracht 1. Noteer deze vergelijkingen in cijfers.

Opdracht 2. In de vergelijking *rubʕ* + *ʕašart itsāʕ* = *sabaʕt isdās* ontbreekt één teken. Welk teken is dat?

Noot: De letters *x* en *š* worden ongeveer als de Nederlandse *ch* en *sj* uitgesproken; *ʕ* is een specifieke Arabische medeklinker. Het streepje boven een klinker geeft lengte aan.

(Ivan Derzhanski)

1st IOL: Borovetz '03. Individual Contest

Problem 2 (25 marks)

Below you see arithmetic equalities written in Egyptian Arabic[1]. All summands, as well as all sums except the last one, are represented as fractions in which neither the numerators nor the denominators are greater than 10, nor is any denominator equal to 1:

tumn + *tumnēn* = *talatt itmān* (1)

sabaʕt itlāt + *suds* = *ʕašart irbāʕ* (2)

tusʕēn + *tusʕ* = *sudsēn* (3)

xamast ixmās + *subʕ* = *tamant isbāʕ* (4)

subʕēn + *xumsēn* = $\frac{24}{35}$ (5)

Assignment 1. Write these equalities in figures.

Assignment 2. The equality *rubʕ* + *ʕašart itsāʕ* = *sabaʕt isdās* is missing a sign. Which one?

Note: The letter *š* is pronounced as English *sh*, *x* as the *ch* in *loch*; *ʕ* is a specific Arabic consonant. A bar above a vowel indicates length. (Ivan Derzhanski)

Figure 1. Half a page from the Dutch and the English versions of the IOL1 problem set.

```
\newpage
\problem {25}
%
Hieronder staan rekenkundige
vergelijkingen in het Egyptische dialect van het Arabisch%
\footnote{[...]}.
%
Alle onderdelen voor en na het ``='' teken zijn breuken waarin de tellers
en noemers niet hoger zijn dan~$10$. (Alleen het rechterdeel van de laatste
som is hierop een uitzondering.) Er is ook geen noemer, die gelijk is aan
$1$:
%
\fracdata
%
\assignment Noteer deze vergelijkingen in cijfers.
\assignment In de vergelijking \hfill \fractest \hfill ontbreekt \'e\'en
teken.\\ Welk teken is dat?
\comment
De letters \wipa x en \wipa{\sh} worden ongeveer als de Nederlandse
\word{ch} en \word{sj} uitgesproken;
\wipa C is een specifieke Arabische medeklinker.
Het streepje boven een klinker geeft lengte aan.
\by{(Ivan Derzhanski)}
```

```
\def \probword {Opgave}
\def \asgtword {Opdracht}
\def \comment {\paragraph {Noot:}}
```

```
\newpage
\problem {25}
%
Below you see arithmetic equalities
written in Egyptian Arabic%
\footnote{[...]}.
%
All summands, as well as all sums except the last one, are represented as
fractions in which neither the numerators nor the denominators are greater
than~$10$, nor is any denominator equal to~$1$:
%
\fracdata
%
\assignment Write these equalities in figures.
\assignment The equality \hfill \fractest \hfill is missing a sign.\\ Which
one?
\comment
The letter \wipa{\sh} is pronounced as English \word{sh}, \wipa x as the
\word{ch} in \word{loch};
\wipa C is a specific Arabic consonant.
A bar above a vowel indicates length.
\by{(Ivan Derzhanski)}
```

```
\def \probword {Problem}
\def \asgtword {Assignment}
\def \comment {\paragraph {Note:}}
```

```
\newcommand \problem [1]{\section*{\probword\ \stepcounter
  {section}\thesection\ (#1 \pontword)}}
\newcommand \assignment {\stepcounter {assignment}\paragraph
  {\asgtword~\theassignment.}}

\def \fractest {$\egar{rubC} + \egar{Ca{\sh}art its\A C} \; = \;
  \egar{sabaCt isd\A s}$}
```

Figure 2. Some excerpts from the Dutch and the English master files and the macro file.

language version and a file of common macro definitions, input by all master files.

Figure 2 shows how this works. The excerpts from the master files generate the text of the problem seen in Figure 1. Both master files refer to the shared macro file for the set of equalities in the data (`\fracdata`) and the equality in the assignment (`\fractest`). The macro file also takes care of the uniformity of the formatting of problems and assignments, although the words for 'Problem' and 'Assignment' in the respective languages are defined in the master files (`\probword` and `\asgtword`).

The same technique saves repetition within each text, for example, when handling a very common form of assignment:

```
\def \fordword #1{Vertaal in het #1}

\assignment \fordword {Nederlands}:        [twice (in Problem 1 and in Problem 4)]
\assignment \fordword {Baskisch}:
\assignment \fordword {Adygisch}:
\assignment \fordword {Adygisch}, op alle mogelijke manieren:
```

```
\def \fordword #1{Translate into #1}

\assignment \fordword {English}:           [twice (as above)]
\assignment \fordword {Basque}:
\assignment \fordword {Adyghe}:
\assignment \fordword {Adyghe} in all possible ways:
```

Figure 3. Some more excerpts from the Dutch and the English master files for IOL1.

The system made the production of the six parallel problem sets significantly more efficient and reliable than if six separate documents had been written. Still, much material is shared by the source files, and as can be seen from Figure 1, the texts in Dutch and in English differ more than they need to.

3 The Present: IOL6 and onwards

The problem sets for IOL2–5 were prepared in Microsoft Word as separate documents, and the identity of the unknown language material as well as the equivalence of the Solverese texts was checked entirely by human eye and hand. By the time the LaTeX-based multilingual system was revived (in 2008), things had changed in several respects. The number of participants in IOL had grown significantly, as had the quantity and diversity of the working languages; IOL itself had become more mature, and harder problems were being assigned; most importantly, the awareness of IOL's Problem Committee of the need to invest more time and attention into the preparation of the problem set (Derzhanski *et al.*, 2004) had increased. But with only so many days in the year, this all meant that the multilingual process often had to start before the content of the problems had been finalised, with changes sometimes proving necessary as an effect of this process, as it emerged that some problems (or parts of them), especially problems involving word semantics, would be easier, or certain explanations make more sense, in some languages than in others.[4] And having to make the same content change in several parallel texts is undesirable, for obvious reasons.

Therefore when the system came back to life in the weeks before IOL6, it did so as its own antithesis. In the new version, which has been in use ever since, the main source files for the individual Solverese versions are very brief. Apart from setting the paper size and the encodings and invoking the Babel package (Braams, 2008) with the appropriate language settings, each inputs two other files. One is composed entirely of macro definitions; this is effectively a pseudocode-to-Solverese dictionary. The other is the text of the problems (statements and solutions), the same for all versions, written entirely in the said pseudocode.

[4] Several early versions of Problem IOL10#5 (on Rotuman, by Boris Iomdin and Alexander Piperski) required the solver to make the conjecture that in Rotuman the word for 'grey' is derived from the word for 'ashes', but this word was removed from the assignment at the final stage, when it was brought to the Problem Committee's attention that the same is true of three of IOL10's working languages.

The canonical solution of Problem IOL5#3 (on Georgian verb morphology, by Yakov Testelets), first composed in Russian, suggested that *predsedatel'stvovat'* was too long a word to gloss a suppletive Georgian verb; this was crossed out because the corresponding verb in English, *chair*, is arguably only two phonemes long.

The original Russian text of Problem IOL1#1 (on Jacob Linzbach's Transcendental Algebra, by Ksenia Gilyarova) glossed the verb ♥ in the same way (*ljubit'*) whether it referred to loving people or liking things, but the final version used different expressions because in Estonian there was no other choice.

Opgave Nr 3 (20 punten). Gegeven zijn enkele zinnen in het Baskisch evenals hun vertalingen in het Nederlands in willekeurige volgorde. Een van de Nederlandse zinnen correspondeert met twee zinnen in het Baskisch:

ahaztu ditut, ahaztu zaizkit, ahaztu zaizu, hurbildu natzaizue, hurbildu zait, lagundu ditugu, lagundu dituzu, lagundu dute, lagundu nauzue, mintzatu natzaizu, mintzatu gatzaizkizue, mintzatu zaizkigu, ukitu ditugu, ukitu naute

jij vergat hem, zij spraken met ons, ik naderde jullie, ik sprak met jou, wij hielpen hen, jullie hielpen mij, hij naderde mij, wij raakten hen aan, zij raakten mij aan, jij hielp hen, zij hielpen hem, wij spraken met jullie, ik vergat hen

(a) Bepaal wat bij elkaar hoort.

(b) Vertaal naar het Baskisch: jij raakte mij aan, zij naderden mij.

(c) Vertaal naar het Nederlands: ***lagundu dut***, ***hurbildu gatzaizkizu***.

(d) Een van de Nederlandse zinnen kan ook op een andere manier worden vertaald naar het Baskisch. Bepaal welke zin dat is en geef de andere mogelijke vertaling.

—*Natalya Zaika*

Problem #3 (20 points). Here are some sentences in Basque as well as their English translations in arbitrary order. One of the English sentences corresponds to two sentences in Basque:

ahaztu ditut, ahaztu zaizkit, ahaztu zaizu, hurbildu natzaizue, hurbildu zait, lagundu ditugu, lagundu dituzu, lagundu dute, lagundu nauzue, mintzatu natzaizu, mintzatu gatzaizkizue, mintzatu zaizkigu, ukitu ditugu, ukitu naute

you_{sg} forgot him, they talked to us, I approached you_{pl}, I talked to you_{sg}, we helped them, you_{pl} helped me, he approached me, we touched them, they touched me, you_{sg} helped them, they helped him, we talked to you_{pl}, I forgot them

(a) Determine the correct correspondences.

(b) Translate into Basque: you_{sg} touched me, they approached me.

(c) Translate into English: ***lagundu dut***, ***hurbildu gatzaizkizu***.

(d) One of the English sentences can be translated into Basque in one more way. Identify this sentence and give the other possible translation.

—*Natalya Zaika*

בעיה מס׳ 3 (20 נקודות). להלן משפטים בשפה הבסקית ותרגומיהם לעברית בערבוביה. אחד המשפטים בעברית תואם שני משפטים בבסקית:

ahaztu ditut, ahaztu zaizkit, ahaztu zaizu, hurbildu natzaizue, hurbildu zait, lagundu ditugu, lagundu dituzu, lagundu dute, lagundu nauzue, mintzatu natzaizu, mintzatu gatzaizkizue, mintzatu zaizkigu, ukitu ditugu, ukitu naute

שכחת ממנו, הם דיברו אתנו, ניגשתי אליכם, דיברתי אתך, עזרנו להם, עזרתם לי, הוא ניגש אלי, נגענו בהם, הם נגעו בי, עזרת להם, הם עזרו לו, דיברנו אתכם, שכחתי מהם

(א) קבעו את ההתאמות הנכונות.

(ב) תרגמו לשפה הבסקית: נגעת בי, הם ניגשו אלי.

(ג) תרגמו לעברית: ***lagundu dut***, ***hurbildu gatzaizkizu***.

(ד) אחד המשפטים בעברית ניתן לתרגום לשפה הבסקית בדרך אחת נוספת. מצאו את המשפט הזה וציינו את התרגום האפשרי השני.

—נטליה זאיקה

Figure 4. Half a page from the Dutch, English and Hebrew versions of the IOL10 problem set.

```
\problem \givesent {\inlgEus} \andtrans {\tothislang} \chaotict. \pasoreus:
%
\begin{center}
\bord{ahaztu ditut, ahaztu zaizkit, ahaztu zaizu, hurbildu natzaizue,
hurbildu zait, lagundu ditugu, lagundu dituzu, lagundu dute,
lagundu nauzue, mintzatu natzaizu, mintzatu gatzaizkizue,
mintzatu zaizkigu, ukitu ditugu, ukitu naute}\medskip

\ahazty 23, \mintzaty 64, \hurbildy 15, \mintzaty 12, \lagundy 46,
\lagundy 51, \hurbildy 31, \ukity 46, \ukity 61, \lagundy 26,
\lagundy 63, \mintzaty 45, \ahazty 16
\end{center}
%
\begin{assgts}
\item \corrcorr.
\item \fordinto {\tolgEus}: \ukity 21, \hurbildy 61.
\item \fordinto {\tothislang}:
  \bord{lagundu dut}, \bord{hurbildu gatzaizkizu}.
\item \formahat {\tolgEus}. \findtran.
\end{assgts}
%
\by{-\NZname}
```

```
\def \givesent #1{Gegeven zijn enkele zinnen in het #1}
\def \andtrans #1{evenals hun vertalingen in het #1}
\def \chaotict{in willekeurige volgorde}
\def \fordinto #1{Vertaal naar het #1}

\def \inlgEus{Baskisch}
\def \tolgEus{Baskisch}
\def \tothislang{Nederlands}

\def \mintzaty #1#2{\iN{#1} sprak\iJ{#1} met \iA{#2}}
\def \ukity #1#2{\iN{#1} raakte\6#1(,,,n,n,n) \iA{#2} aan}

\def \iN #1{\6#1(ik,jij,hij,wij,jullie,zij)}
\def \iA #1{\6#1(mij,jou,hem,ons,jullie,hen)}
\def \iJ #1{\6#1(,,,en,en,en)}
```

```
\def \givesent #1{Here are some sentences in #1}
\def \andtrans #1{as well as their #1 translations}
\def \chaotict{in arbitrary order}
\def \fordinto #1{Translate into #1}

\def \inlgEus{Basque}
\def \tolgEus{Basque}
\def \tothislang{English}

\def \mintzaty #1#2{\iN{#1} talked
to \iA{#2}}
\def \ukity #1#2{\iN{#1} touched \iA{#2}}

\def \iN #1{\6#1(I,y\ous,he,we,y\oup,they)}
\def \iA #1{\6#1(me,y\ous,him,us,y\oup,them)}
```

In the English master file:

```
\def \ous {ou$_{\textrm{\small sg}}$}
\def \oup {ou$_{\textrm{\small pl}}$}
```

Figure 5. Excerpts from the pseudocode source and the Dutch and English dictionaries.

Figure 4 presents half a page from the Dutch, English and Hebrew versions of the IOL10 problem set; Figure 5, the text of this problem in pseudocode and some excerpts from the Dutch and English dictionary files.

How much granularity is desirable depends on the variety of the data and the regularity of the relevant fragments of the grammars of the featured and the working languages. Breaking down a sentence such as *He ate the fish* (and its equivalents) into subject, verb and object and generating each by its own macro makes the most sense if the same constituents also appear elsewhere in the text, but it always makes verification easier.

One important advantage of this approach over the others was already noted: if a content change in some problem (adding, replacing or deleting some item in the data or the assignments) is required, it is made in one place only, reducing the danger of error. Another lies in the making of the dictionaries. Those are prepared by filling the cells of a spreadsheet, with all languages in parallel columns. Figure 6 shows a screenshot containing part of the spreadsheet for IOL10 (several rows and six of the 15 working languages).

	RU	NL	EN	RO	HU	HE
givesent #1	Даны предложения н	Gegeven zijn enkele z	Here are some sentenc	Sunt date propoziții îr	Adva vannak mondato	להלן משפטים ב#1
andtrans #1	и их переводы на #1	evenals hun vertalinge	as well as their #1 trar	şi traducerile lor în #1	valamint fordításuk #:	ותרגומיהם ל#1
chaotict	в перепутанном поря	in willekeurige volgoı	in arbitrary order	în ordine arbitrară	véletlen sorrendben	בערבוביה
fordinto #1	Переведите на #1	Vertaal naar het #1	Translate into #1	Traduceţi în #1	Fordítsa le #1	תרגמו ל#1
inlgEus	баскском языке	Baskisch	Basque	limba bască	baszk nyelven	שפה הבסקית
tolgEus	баскский язык	Baskisch	Basque	limba bască	baszkra	שפה הבסקית
tothislang	русский язык	Nederlands	English	română	magyarra	עברית
mintzaty #1#	\iN{#1} говорил\ifnu	\iN{#1} sprak\iJ{#1}	\iN{#1} talked to \iA{	\iN{#1} \iJ{#1} vorbi	\iN{#1} beszélt\iJ{#1	\iN{#1}דיבר\iJ{#1} ת
ukity #1#2	\iN{#1} дотронул\ifr	\iN{#1} raakte\6#1(,,	\iN{#1} touched \iA{	\iN{#1} \iA{#2}-\iJ{	\iN{#1} \iA{#2} nyúl	\iN{#1}נגע\iJ{#1} ב\i
iN #1	\6#1(я,ты,он,мы,вы,(	\6#1(ik,jij,hij,wij,julli	\6#1(I,y\ous,he,we,y\c	\6#1(eu,tu,el,noi,voi,(	\6#1(én,te,ő,mi,ti,ők)	\ifxהוא3#1 \else\ifxהם
paani #1#2	\Uppcase \iN{#1} съе	\Uppcase \iN{#1} he\	\Uppcase \iN{#1} ate	\Uppcase \iN{#1} \iJ{	Megett\6#1(em,ed,e,ü	\iN{#1}אכל\iJ{#1} #2
bonaiana	рыбу	de vis	the fish	peştele	a halat	את הדג
bonaover	кокос	de kokosnoot	the coconut	nuca de cocos	a kókuszt	את הקוקוס

Figure 6. A screenshot of part of the multilingual spreadsheet.

This makes it easy to compare words or sentences in any two languages and to find mismatches and imbalances. Also, since the ordering of the rows of the spreadsheet is immaterial, they can be arranged and rearranged to group certain words or sentences in close rows in order to make similarities or differences stand out.[5]

A final advantage is the move away from the model (disadvantageous for more than one reason[6]) in which the version of a problem in one working language is the original and the other versions are translations. The parallel production of all Solverese versions from the same pseudocode source and with use of dictionaries made from a table where all working languages are uniformly situated creates the effect of (machine) translation from pseudocode to all languages, which in turn makes all languages equal. At a contest such as IOL, where all contestants are to have the same chances regardless of their working languages, this is of vital importance.

The method has been tested and proven to work with two Cyrillic-written and 12 Roman-written languages, as well as Korean (at IOL7) and Hebrew (at IOL10), with hardly any technical difficulties. It remains to be seen whether it will meet just as cheerfully the predictable further growth of the number and diversity of IOL's working languages, but it is certain that its potential has not yet been fully explored.

[5] One of the phenomena in Problem IOL10#1 (on Dyirbal, by Artūrs Semeņuks) was factitive morphology; it was illustrated by several deadjectival verbs, which could be translated as lexical factitives (*bent* → *bend*, *healthy* → *heal*) or as periphrastic ones (*fat* → *make fat*, *sleep* → *make fall asleep*), but which were which differed from one working language to the other. In order to guarantee the equal difficulty of the problem in all versions it was necessary to ensure that each language used factitives of several types, which was facilitated by the summary character of the spreadsheet.

[6] At IOL5, where some versions of the problem set were made by translating the English one, the sentence 'Knowledge of English is not necessary for solving the problem' was supposed to be present in one of the problems, but was omitted from the English version (because of its obvious inappropriateness there) and therefore didn't make it into the other ones either; this was considered a grave mishap.

References

B. Bozhanov and I. Derzhanski. 2013. Rosetta Stone Linguistic Problems. In this volume.

Johannes Braams. 2008. Babel, a multilingual package for use with LaTeX's standard document classes. CTAN:macros/latex/required/babel/.

I.A. Derzhanski, A.S. Berdichevsky, K.A. Gilyarova, B.L. Iomdin, E.V. Muravenko, and M.L. Rubinstein. 2004. On the Translatability of Linguistic Problems: the Lessons of the First International Linguistics Olympiad. In: I.M. Kobozeva, A.S. Narinyani, and V.P. Selegey (eds.), *Proceedings of the International Conference Dialogue 2004: Computational Linguistics and Intellectual Technologies*. Nauka, Moscow, 166–171 (in Russian).

Ivan A. Derzhanski. 2009. *Linguistic Magic and Mystery*. Union of Bulgarian Mathematicians, Sofia.

I.A. Derzhanski and T.E. Payne. 2009. The Linguistics Olympiads: Academic competitions in linguistics for secondary school students. In: K. Denham and A. Lobeck (eds.), *Linguistics at School: Language Awareness in Primary and Secondary Education*, Cambridge University Press, Cambridge, UK, 213–226.

Donald E. Knuth. 1986. *The TEXbook*. Addison–Wesley, Reading, MA.

Learning from OzCLO, the Australian Computational and Linguistics Olympiad

Dominique Estival
U. of Western Sydney
d.estival@uws.edu.au

John Henderson
U. of Western Australia
john.henderson@uwa.edu.au

Mary Laughren
U. of Queensland
m.laughren@uq.edu.au

Diego Mollá
Macquarie U.
diego.molla-aliod@mq.edu.au

Cathy Bow
Charles Darwin U.
cathy.bow@cdu.edu.au

Rachel Nordlinger
U. of Melbourne
racheln@unimelb.edu.au

Verna Rieschild
Macquarie U.
verna.rieschild@mq.edu.au

Andrea C. Schalley
Griffith U.
a.schalley@griffith.edu.au

Alexander W. Stanley
Macquarie U.
alexander.stanley@students.mq.edu.au

Colette Mrowa-Hopkins
Flinders U.
colette.mrowa-hopkins@flinders.edu.au

Abstract

The Australian Computational and Linguistics Olympiad (OzCLO) started in 2008 in only two locations and has since grown to a nationwide competition with almost 1500 high school students participating in 2013. An Australian team has participated in the International Linguistics Olympiad (ILO) every year since 2009. This paper describes how the competition is run (with a regional First Round and a final National Round) and the organisation of the competition (a National Steering Committee and Local Organising Committees for each region) and discusses the particular challenges faced by Australia (timing of the competition and distance between the major population centres). One major factor in the growth and success of OzCLO has been the introduction of the online competition, allowing participation of students from rural and remote country areas. The organisation relies on the good-will and volunteer work of university and school staff but the strong interest among students and teachers shows that OzCLO is responding to a demand for linguistic challenges.

1 Introduction

The Australian Computational and Linguistic Olympiad (OzCLO, www.ozclo.org.au) began as an idea in late 2007, largely prompted by a parent in Ballarat, a small town in Victoria, who came across the North American competition (NACLO, Radev et al. 2008) on the internet and thought it was something that her daughter would be interested in doing. Her emails to the organisers of NACLO, asking about the likelihood of such an event being run in Australia, led to initiating contact with the Australasian Language Technology Association (ALTA) with the suggestion that a computational linguistic olympiad be established in Australia. Dominique Estival (then at Appen Pty Ltd, and a member of the ALTA Steering Committee) took on the project and, jointly with Jane Simpson (then from the University of Sydney), Rachel Nordlinger and Jean Mulder (from the University of Melbourne), ran the first ever Australian Computational and Linguistic Olympiad in 2008, with financial support from HCSNet (the Human Communication Science Network), and help from ALTA (the Australasian Language Technology Association), ALS (the Australian Linguistic Society) and CSIRO (the Commonwealth Scientific and Industrial Research Organisation). The first competition was held in two locations – the University of Melbourne (Victoria) and the University of Sydney (New South Wales) – with a total of 119 students participating from 22 schools. Given the success of this first competition, 2009 saw the addition of four new locations around Australia (Adelaide, South Australia; Brisbane, Queensland; Canberra, ACT; Perth, Western Australia) and the sending of the national winning team to the International Linguistic Olympiad in Wroclaw, Poland. Since then OzCLO has run every year, with the recent addition of two regions (NSW-North in 2010 and Northern Territory in 2013) and the participation of an Australian team in every ILO.

2 Philosophy, Aims and Principles

The immediate aim of OzCLO (Simpson and Henderson, 2010) is to introduce high school students to language puzzles from which they can learn about the richness, diversity and systematic nature of language, and develop their reasoning skills. The general value of this type of knowledge and skills in high school education has not been specifically articulated to potential participants or their teachers, schools or parents, as it has in the UK (UKLO, 2011; Hudson and Sheldon, 2013). However, informal feedback and the participation rate both indicate a widespread perception in the school sector that this type of activity has educational value, albeit with different focuses in different schools. For many of the schools that participate, OzCLO provides a means to meet their institutional responsibility to provide extra-curricular activities that are intellectually stimulating and broadening for academically high-achieving students (under rubrics such as 'gifted and talented'). Some schools offer OzCLO to a wider range of students.

The broader aim of OzCLO is to promote awareness of, and interest in linguistics and computational linguistics in high schools and in the wider community, and more specifically to increase enrolments in these disciplines at university level. A further goal is that this will ultimately attract people to careers in these areas. Linguistics has traditionally had little recognition at high school level in Australia, even within language education, although more recently there is linguistics content at upper high school level in the English Language course in Victoria and in the new national English curriculum. OzCLO has been running in most regions long enough to see participants reaching university, and although there has been no proper research on the impact of OzCLO on enrolments, there is anecdotal evidence that some former participants have chosen to study at least some linguistics.

Consistent with the key aim of promoting interest, OzCLO operates on the principles that participation should be fun and should offer achievable if challenging tasks to a wide range of students across science and humanities interests, especially in the First Round. Schools are provided with a training package of problems which starts with a simple morphological analysis that is suitable to do as a whole-class exercise even if they do not proceed to the competition itself. In both rounds participation takes place in school-based teams, rather than individual competition. This is partly to encourage students to learn to communicate their analytical ideas, to collaborate effectively, and to provide mutual support and social interaction. It also offers some organisational advantages in terms of registration and marking. Because team members may have different levels of ability, the competition process does not necessarily identify the highest achieving individuals, but this risk is out-weighed by the benefits of teams. The organisation of the First Round as separate competitions in each region provides each team with a smaller pool to compete in initially and a distinct level of local achievement. However, since there are considerable differences in the number of teams in each region, and the top teams from each region are invited into the National Round, the national competition does not necessarily consist of the highest achieving teams nationally and there is currently discussion of methods to minimise this effect. Finally, the results are structured to recognise participation as well as high achievement: in addition to recognising the top teams, all teams receive certificates in the categories Gold (top ≈25%), Silver (next ≈25%) and Bronze (remainder).

3 Organising the Annual Competition

3.1 University level

All Australian states and territories (with the exception of Tasmania) now participate in OzCLO and there is typically one Local Organising Committee (LOC) for each geographical region. There are currently eight LOCs (soon to be nine with the addition of a third New South Wales region). Each LOC has the responsibility for student and school liaison, university space booking, recruiting volunteer academic and student helpers, running the competitions, publicising the event locally, and finding cash or in-kind sponsorship (e.g. for rooms, venues, printing and prizes).

The National Steering Committee (NSC) comprises the Chair of each LOC, the Problems Coordinator, the Treasurer, the OZCLO Webmaster and the Online Competition Coordinator. The NSC's role is to coordinate between LOCs, make and implement OzCLO decisions, and coordinate national sponsorships and publicity. A training package is developed by the NSC and provided online each year, on the OzCLO website and within the online competition site. The NSC Chair has the responsibility of ensuring the coordination and execution of tasks for OzCLO, both nationally and internationally. The NSC Chair and the Problems Coordinator liaise with ELCLO (English Linguistics and Computational Linguistics Olympiads) with regard to developing annual problem sets, and with the International Linguistics Olympiad (ILO/IOL) with regard to the international competition. NSC members may have dual responsibilities.

Because of the distances between regional centres, the NSC meetings are all conducted via teleconferences, and committee members share documents and records using Airset, a cloud-based collaboration site.

3.2 School level

OzCLO operates on a democratic basis, with the devolution of decision making passing from NSC to LOC to school teacher to students. Teacher and student feedback often contributes to NSC discussions. Information is disseminated to school teachers through the website as well as through emails from the region's LOC. This information is also shared via Facebook and Twitter accounts. Training sessions are provided online, at universities and, in some cases, within schools. Teachers register teams of 4 members at the Junior (Years 9 and 10) or Senior level (Years 11-12) online. There is no limit to registrations for the online competition, but registrations for the offline competition (in which students typically attend the organising University campus) may be constrained by University venue availability issues. Some schools have Linguistics Clubs, and OzCLO is a strong focus for their activities. In some regions, schools with over 80 participating students request in-house training and invigilation for an offline First Round.

3.3 The public face of OzCLO

OzCLO has a website (www.ozclo.org.au) and a social media presence with Twitter and Facebook accounts for communications and promotion. Most LOCs have been successful in gaining publicity for OzCLO through their University media departments. Many schools publish pictures and items about OzCLO achievements in their school newsletters. Some individual schools have featured in the local press after results of competitions have been published. OzCLO has also featured in national radio segments.

4 The OzCLO Competition

4.1 Competitions Rounds

The OzCLO competition consists of two rounds, a regional or state-wide First Round and a National Round. In both, school-based teams of up to four students attempt to solve five or six linguistic problems in two hours. The teams are divided into Senior and Junior sections, with the Senior teams drawn from the last two years of high school (Tears 11 and 12) while the Junior teams are drawn from the two preceding years (Years 9 and 10). The same problems sets and competition conditions hold for both Senior and Junior teams. The top three teams from each LOC are invited to go on to the National Round which is held under the same conditions. If the top Junior team is not in the overall top three teams, then it is also invited. The Senior team which wins the National Round is invited to represent Australia at the ILO.

4.2 Problem sets

In its first two years, OzCLO greatly benefited from NACLO, which allowed use of their problem sets. Some additional problems were composed by linguists engaged in the running of the competition, or their colleagues. Since 2009, OzCLO has been part of ELCLO, the English Language Computational Linguistics Olympiad, in which participating countries (Australia, Ireland, North America and the United Kingdom) contribute to a shared set of problems. Because of the OzCLO rationale described above, an attempt is made to try to have a mix of problems based on data from a wide range of languages, and also a wide range of data types. Different levels of difficulty are included so that students have the satisfaction of being able to solve most of the problems. The aim is to show students that analysing language phenomena can be fun as well as challenging, and also that linguistic skills can be applied to some very practical tasks. The problems include: deciphering non-Roman scripts; translation tasks involving typical morphological and syntactic analysis; computational linguistic tasks; search for phonological rules, or linguistic reconstruction.

4.3 Training for ILO

Since 2009, an Australian team has participated in every ILO. While the main goal of OzCLO has always been the promotion of language studies, linguistic knowledge and analysis skills in

Australian high schools, the appeal of potentially participating in an international competition has proved an additional incentive for many of the students and their teachers. However, because of the rationale for OzCLO discussed above, the problems used in the First Round and even the National Round are not nearly as difficult as the actual ILO problems. Therefore the Australian team needs to be given additional training before competing at the international level. This training was first provided by a coach accompanying the team at the ILO but we have found that this was insufficient and too late to be helpful. We now provide training sessions aimed at solving ILO-level problems to the winning team prior to travelling to the ILO. This has resulted in higher results, including an individual silver medal in 2011 and honourable mentions in 2010 and 2012.

5 Participation 2008-2013

OzCLO has evolved from 22 schools and 119 competing students in 2008 to 87 schools and 1,451 competing students in 2013. Some schools have participated each year, and there has been a steady increase in new schools. Private and selective government schools have so far been the majority in most regions, but the numbers of government schools participating are growing. All participating schools are highly enthusiastic about the OzCLO competitions.

OzCLO naturally attracts schools keen on offering a new kind of challenge to students in their GATS (gifted and talented students) programmes. However, teachers (not only language teachers, but also mathematics and computer sciences teachers) also comment that OzCLO is a rare kind of competition because it provides fun, challenge, stimulation and team work for any student.

A challenge for Australia compared with Europe or North America is the enormous distance between rural and metropolitan areas, making it difficult for many schools in rural areas to participate in an offline University-based competition. The advent of the online option gives urban, rural and country remote students equity in access. Thanks to this plus a strong marketing drive in that state, numbers have increased dramatically in Queensland. In other regions, some schools prefer the university campus experience offered by the offline option.

As Table 1 shows, numbers have increased steadily over the six years since inception. In 2013, Australia's population of 23 million has provided nearly as many Linguistics Olympiads competitors as has the United States and Canada combined, whose population figures are fifteen times more than Australia's. The OzCLO participation rate is 6.4 per 100,000 population. For UKLO it is 4.55, and for NACLO 0.49.

6 Going on-line

In the first four years of OzCLO's existence, the competition was offered on campus by academic staff volunteers from a number of mainly metropolitan Universities. Participating teams travelled from their schools to the respective Universities' campuses to take part in the Training Session and the First Round, except for NSW, where several OzCLO representatives also travelled to schools with a large participation base, in order to run the competition at the school. Teachers often reported that these visits to the University campus were a highlight for the participating students who very much enjoyed the experience.

Nonetheless, a number of drawbacks to this approach became apparent quite early. These included:

- The difficulty of organising suitable venues on campus for running the competition due to the timing of the First Round (usually coinciding with Universities' Orientation Week or their first weeks of teaching in the first semester).
- The distance factor with the result that only schools within travel distance could participate in the competition (in the case of Queensland, for instance, no school beyond a distance of about 100kms from campus participated in the offline competition). Given the size of Australia, most regional and rural schools were thus virtually excluded from competing.
- Constraints on availability of venues and markers put a cap on the overall number of students who could compete in each region. Thus, the number of schools and the number of students per school had to be limited by the local committees from the outset (e.g. in Queensland, only two teams per school were able to compete, although some schools wished to enrol many more).

LOC	2008 Schools/ students	2009 Schools/ Students	2010 Schools/ students	2011 Schools/ students	2012 Schools/ students	2013 Schools/ students	Region population 000s	Participants per 100,000 population
NSW-S	10 64	14 105	[fn/a] 92	15 279	12 289	9 312	7,314	5.24
NSW-N	n/a	n/a	5 40	7 58	5 60	6 71		
VIC	12 55	11 90	[fn/a] 120	9 115	16 245	18 304	5,649	5.38
ACT	n/a	7 30	5 83	5 72	9 136	9 161	377	42.76
QLD	n/a	11 60	15 90	15 106	20 312	25 377	4,585	8.22
SA	n/a	[fn/a] 29	5 33	3 19	4 27	3 34	1,658	2.05
NT	n/a	n/a	n/a	n/a	n/a	6 80	236	33.86
WA	n/a	10 78	11 144	16 143	14 120	12 120	2,451	4.90
TAS	n/a	n/a	n/a	n/a	n/a	n/a	512	0
Overall	119 students	392 students	602 students	792 students	1069 students	1459 students	22,786	6.40

Table 1: Participation schools/students
(n/a = not applicable = LOC was not participating; [fn/a] =figure not available

In order to address these issues, it was decided to offer an online option in 2012, using Griffith University's Learning Management System. This lifted restrictions on numbers (both school and students per school), and schools were able to compete from anywhere in Australia if they so wished. As a result, schools located as far as 1,500 kms from the metropolitan areas have successfully participated in the competition, and some schools registered more than 20 teams in the latest competition. With the online option, the overall number of participants has increased dramatically (see Table 2). For instance, Victoria saw the number of their participants double from 2011 to 2012, while numbers in Queensland nearly tripled. Even in those regions that shifted to exclusively offering the online option (such as Queensland in the last two years), most schools have remained in the competition.

	2012		2013	
LOC	Online students	On campus students	Online Students	On-campus Students
NSW-S	91	198	120	192
NSW-N	60	[on/a]	8	63
VIC	137	108	195	109
ACT	64	72	115	46
QLD	312	[on/a]	377	on/a
SA	0	27	34	on/a
WA	28	92	120	on/a
NT	n/a	n/a	80	on/a

Table 2: Participation numbers by mode (online/on-campus)
(n/a = not applicable (LOC was not participating); [fn/a] =figure not available;
[on/a] =option not available)

In terms of students competing online vs. on-campus, except for the NSW-N region, there is a distinct shift towards participating online. Feedback from teachers has shown that in many cases it is easier for teams to stay within the school grounds for the competition rather than to travel to the University campus. For some schools, however, travelling to the University campus is still one of the major benefits they would not want to lose. For this reason most LOCs offer both on-campus and online options. Some regions choose to only offer the online option (with a training session at the University).

Teams participating online have access to training materials and all the necessary information, which is made available through the OzCLO website well before the competition day. This site also allows teams to familiarise themselves with the online testing system. On the day, all teams across Australia compete at the same time on the same day and within the same two hour period (to compensate for time zone differences, teams started at 12:00 in WA, 13:30 in the NT, 14:00 in QLD, 14:30pm in SA and 15:00 in the ACT, NSW and VIC in the 2013 competition).

In terms of process and technical requirements, each participating team needs access to an Internet-enabled computer on the day of the competition. No special software is required on the school's computers. The problem set is made available to teachers shortly before the competition commences, in order to allow them to print and copy the problems for the students. Students usually work on the paper copy, and then access the computer to enter their responses. There is also a virtual classroom set up for live communication during the competition, in order to allow students and teachers to ask questions but also to show students that there are hundreds of competitors participating from around the country at the same time.

Overall, the addition of the online alternative has been a very beneficial development for OzCLO. The strong growth in overall participant numbers over recent years is not simply due to the online option, but this has certainly played a major role. It remains to be seen if there is even more potential for growth – especially in areas outside of the major cities.

7 Challenges

One of the main challenges OzCLO faces is the timing of the competition in relation to the schedule of the international linguistics competitions. The Australian school year begins in February and ends in December, and the university year is roughly March to November, in contrast to the September-June academic calendars of the northern hemisphere. In order for an Australian team to be selected with enough time to prepare for participation in the ILO, the National Round needs to be held before the Easter break (March/April). For Universities and schools, this creates a very rushed timeline at the busiest time of the school/academic year.

As mentioned earlier, another challenge for Australia is the vast distances between metropolitan areas, where most of the universities are located. In spite of the success of the online competition, so far OzCLO has had mostly a metropolitan base and has not yet fully engaged in marketing to regional and rural areas across the whole country. Targeting appropriate teachers within schools can also be a challenge, as experience has shown that often the information does not filter through to the relevant teachers (these are usually the coordinators of Languages, Gifted Education, Mathematics, or Computing programmes). Contacting the professional associations for the different teaching specialties could ensure that information is disseminated more efficiently.

Funding is not guaranteed, and fundraising efforts are not rewarded every year. All organisational efforts at University and school level depend on good-will and volunteering as well as donations. Changes in Heads of Departments in Universities and principals in schools can impact negatively on funds and participation levels. This means that core issues need to be resolved again every year, for example, the ongoing maintenance of the OzCLO website/online registration system, which is both a challenge and a solution to other issues. The OzCLO website hosting is provided by Macquarie University and the site is maintained by a student volunteer. It has served as the central hub of information, with other modes (email, Facebook and Twitter) leading back to it for detailed information. In addition to ordinary information, it also enables self-service registration, and the automated generation of PDF certificates after the competition. These facilities and the volunteer support of the webmaster have significantly lowered the administrative and financial overhead for the organisers.

An additional problem for OzCLO is the division of Australia's most populated state (NSW, with almost a third of Australia's population) into northern and southern regions, which leads to one state providing double the competitors of other states into the National Round. A model is needed whereby all competitors, no matter whether they come from a small or a large region, have an equal opportunity to compete in the National Round.

Finally, while OzCLO has been able to contribute a number of linguistic problems to the ELCLO pool, it has proved extremely difficult to obtain contributions from Computational Linguistics (Estival, 2011).

8 Conclusions

In conclusion, running the OzCLO competition has been an activity well worth the effort, and it is very rewarding that it has become a fixture in the academic calendar for many schools. Students, teachers and principals have been extremely positive about the experience, giving encouraging feedback and expressing strong support for the competition. The recent increases in participation rates have come from new regions (only one Australian state currently has no LOC, but possibilities are being explored in this area), new schools, and larger numbers from individual schools (up to 100 participants from a single school). Some schools have started a linguistics club as after school activity, and others are promoting their experiences on social media.

While there is no data currently available regarding any effect on enrolments in tertiary linguistics programs, increased interest in and awareness of linguistics is certainly a positive outcome for a discipline which faces challenges of funding and viability. The cooperation of academics from universities across the country in all the LOCs and the NSC, plus the support of the Australian Linguistics Society (ALS) and of the Australasian Language Technology Association (ALTA), make the competition a truly national event. This means that the competition is not dependent on any one single person or institution (although competition within particular regions is), and allows for further growth. Ongoing funding and continued support from both universities and schools across the country should see continued growth in the popularity and spread of the competition.

References

Derzhanski, Ivan, and Thomas Payne. (2010). The linguistic olympiads: academic competitions in linguistics for secondary school students. *Linguistics at school: language awareness in primary and secondary education*, ed. By Kristin Denham and Anne Lobeck, 213–26. Cambridge: Cambridge University Press.

Estival, Dominique. (2011). "OzCLO: The Australian Computational Linguistic Olympiad". Proceedings of the Australasian Language Technology Association Workshop 2011. Canberra, Australia.

Hudson, Richard, and Sheldon, Neil. (2013). "Linguistics at School: The UK Linguistics Olympiad." *Language and Linguistics pass*, Volume 7, Issue 2. pp. 91–104,

Radev, Dragomir R., Lori S. Levin, and Thomas E. Payne. (2008). "The North American Computational Linguistics Olympiad (NACLO)". In Proceedings of The Third Workshop on Issues in Teaching Computational Linguistics, Columbus, OH, USA.

Simpson, Jane, and Henderson, John. (2010). Australian Computational and Linguistics Olympiad. Cross Section, Vol. 20, No. 3, July 2010: 10-14.

United Kingdom Linguistics Olympiad Committee. (n.d.) The Linguistics Olympiads: Lots of fun, but are they educational? http://www.uklo.org/?page_id=35.

The Swedish Model of Public Outreach of Linguistics to secondary school Students through Olympiads

Patrik Roos
Young Scientists Stockholm
roos@lingolympiad.org

Hedvig Skirgård
Young Scientists Stockholm
hedvig@lingolympiad.org

Abstract

What is it that we want to achieve with our Linguistic Olympiads and how do the contests vary in different countries? The Swedish Olympiad has been running for 7 years now and is primarily focused on public outreach - spreading linguistics to secondary school students. The contest involves not only a test but also lectures, school visits and teaching material. The effort is put on promoting the interest of linguistics to students through fun material and good contact with teachers of languages. This presentation contains an overview of the Swedish version of Olympiads in Linguistics as well as some concrete examples of workshop material on linguistic problems for secondary school students.

1 Introduction

This paper presents an overview of the way the Olympiad in Linguistics is run in Sweden and how one can go about public outreach of linguistics to secondary school students. This paper and presentation intends to provide useful tips on how an olympiad of this kind can be organised and also discuss how we in the linguistics community can spread linguistics to potential students and the non-academic world.

The Swedish Olympiad in Linguistics (''Lingolympiaden'') started in 2006 as a project within Young Scientists Stockholm. The winners of the Swedish contest have participated in the International Olympiad in Linguistics (IOL) since 2007 and in 2010 Sweden was host country for IOL.

There are a couple of things that set the Swedish contest apart from most other olympiads of linguistics around the world:

1. the contest takes place at the involved universities themselves, not in classrooms in secondary schools
2. the contest is a whole-day event with contest in the morning and lectures in the afternoon
3. there are fewer participants that many other countries participating in IOL
4. the contest has a focus on public outreach rather than finding the best competitors for IOL
5. we engage in other public outreach activities such as school visits, lectures and group assignments for secondary school students
6. the primary audience is secondary school students that study languages, humanities and social science rather than the natural sciences

The aim of Lingolympiaden is to spread linguistics to secondary school students in a fun and educational way. While there are many extra curricular activities for students of the natural sciences: such as the other olympiads, summer schools, exhibitions etc there are relatively few alternatives for students of social sciences. Lingolympiaden intends to fill that void, showing that science does not only consist of the natural sciences and that linguistics is a fun and exciting discipline.

Lingolympiaden is run as a collaborative project between the Young Scientists Stockholm (YSS) and the Linguistics departments at Stockholm University and Lund University. YSS is a youth volunteer organisation devoted to spreading the interest of science and technology to the youth of Sweden (youth $<$26 years old).

Lingolympiaden is funded by the universities, the county council of Stockholm, YSS and The Royal Swedish Academy of Letters, History and Antiquities.

2 The different organisers aims and contributions

The university contributes with rooms and staff for creating and coordinating the problem set as well as correcting.The incentive for the universities to be involved in this is primarily to make secondary school students aware that linguistics exists and potentially acquire more students.

YSS coordinates the entire project, contacts schools, applies for funding etc. YSS also make school visits, talking about linguistics and problems from the olympiads with secondary school students. The goal of YSS is to encourage the youth of Sweden to be interested in science and technology and pursue college studies. YSS receives funding from the County Council of Stockholm for this.

The Royal Swedish Academy of Letters, History and Antiquities funds Sweden's participation in the International contest. The academy is interested in promoting humanities and the social sciences to the youth and as one of the very few enterprises that actually does this Lingolympiaden receives their funding.

As all of the involved parties in Lingolympiaden are interested in promoting linguistics to secondary school students rather than obtaining the highest scores in IOL our contest is more geared towards sparking interest than finding the best problem solvers. Lingolympiaden is more focused on finding secondary school students that are interested in languages and make them interested in social science and linguistics rather than making students that are already interested in natural science and programming interested in languages.

3 Target audience and contact

Lingolympiaden aims to reach secondary school students that are interested in languages and linguistics and encourage them to become interested in studying social sciences, especially linguistics, at university. It has become apparent that students who are interested in the other olympiads and students that are very enthusiastic about natural sciences and programming seem to find the contest even if there has been little effort to reach them. It is much harder to reach secondary school students enrolled in programmes of social sciences and humanities as they are generally less used to there being extra curricular activities for them to be involved in. That being said, Lingolympiaden is of course open to all students (including students of non-theoretical programmes), students from natural science or programming backgrounds are more than welcome - it is just that efforts are put where they seem to be needed (and wanted) the most.

Lingolympiaden would also like to reach more students who come from families with little higher education, but as these students are less likely to choose theoretical secondary school programmes and also less likely to have passionate and driven teachers this has proved a very hard task indeed.

The primary means of contact are teachers of languages at secondary schools. In 2011 the Swedish government initiated a new secondary school programme of humanities that includes a basic course in linguistics as well as more classes in modern languages. We can take no credit for this, however, Lingolympiaden has established a stable and good contact with the Swedish Language Teachers Association as well as with teachers involved in this new secondary school programme. This has been a very fruitful connection, not only in that the contest reaches the students but also because the teachers have benefited from this in their education.

Lingolympiaden also provides teaching materials in form of slides for classes in general linguistics, an IPA tutorial and adapted versions of old problems from the contest. Teachers and students are also able to ask questions about linguistics over email and Lingolympiaden gives advice on literature and sites (WALS, Ethnologue, Universals Archive, MultiTree, Omniglot, LangDoc, UNESCO Atlas of the World's Languages in Danger, The Linguistics Podcasts by LinguistChris, The Five Minute Linguist-podcast etc.) that are useful to the teachers in their education. In addition to this Lingolympiaden visits secondary schools, giving lectures in linguistics and holding workshops on Olympiad problems for a nominal fee. These services are much appreciated by the teachers and students.

Maintaining an active and good relation with the teachers is crucial in recruiting contestants to Lingolympiaden as well as a perfect opportunity to provide our first and foremost goal, to increase the interest in linguistics among the secondary school students.

4 The problems of Lingolympiaden

Lingolympiaden aims to include problems from computational linguistics, general linguistics (primarily grammatical typology), field linguistics, phonetics and psycho linguistics. The staff at the universities are encouraged to construct problems on their area of expertise. Since there are many Ph.D. students who work on language descriptions and linguistic typology at Swedish universities there have been many problems on minor languages such as Kuot of Papua New Guinea and interesting grammatical phenomena such as hodiernal tense. The problem set of the Swedish contest has featured adapted and translated problems from other olympiads and other sources (Speculative Grammarian for example), but as the staff at the universities improve with every year there are less and less of these external problems.

The problem constructors are advised to take into consideration that the problems are to be solvable by secondary school students with no linguistic training, but at the same time the problems shouldn't be based on pure logic alone. This is a tricky balance and it is impossible to make sure that no-one has an unfair advantage.

The problem set for the Swedish olympiad is dependent on who within the university staff has the time to spend construction and testing problems. While the attention is to cover all areas within linguistics it is rare that staff from all sections are able to contribute. This is not a problem that is unique to the Swedish contest, more international collaboration will hopefully improve this situation. Translating Swedish problems into English, Russian, Bulgarian, Italian or German is very feasible.

4.1 Adaptation of problems into teaching material - some examples

When visiting at school it isn't always possible to use problems from the Swedish or International olympiads directly as they were constructed - many problems need to be modified to better suit the conditions of the workshop. When conducting workshops it isn't the aim to test the students but rather to discuss different approaches to the problem and encourage their interest. Here are some examples of the problems that have been used in workshops at secondary schools.

Lingdoku by Trey Jones

Lingdoku is an IPA version of the Japanese number game Sudoku. This is very useful type of problem since most students are already familiar with the premises of Sudoku, it gives them a nice introduction to the variables necessary to define consonants and it is great for illustrating different approaches of problem solving. Since students enrolled in the new humanities programme are required to learn IPA this problem is also much appreciated by teachers.

Lingdoku focuses only on pulmonic consonants and two variables, manner and place. The adaptation used in Lingolympiadens workshop has 4*4 different symbols to place within the grid without repeating the same manner or place in the 4 2*2-squares or any row or column. The Lingdoku table will have some values filled in and by regulating these one can change the time necessary to solve the problem and also change focus on what part of the problem solving we want to emphasise.

Drehu & Cemuhî by Ksenija Giljarova

This problem comes from IOL-6 (2008 in Slanchev Bryag). It has proven to be a highly useful and appreciated problem to run with students. It is quite illustrative of the kind of problems one might encounter and it is not solvable by only applying straightforward logic.

The problem consists of two sets of words in two related languages with translations into Swedish in a scrambled order. There are also a few morphemes that are translated are given as related in the two languages but with no Swedish translation. The method of solving it involves applying several ways of comparing the languages, the students have to be able to identify that the words have developed differently in the two languages and that concepts like horizon, border, wall and beach share a certain semantic component (''boundary''). It serves as inspiration and proof to students that their knowledge, experience and general feel for language and linguistics is directly applicable to solving concrete linguistic problems.

PSG Web Laboratory by Torbjörn Lager

The Linguistics department at Gothenburg University have developed a simple online tool for creating context-free phrase structure grammars and testing them out. It was developed as an aid in a course on generative grammar and CFGs but it has quickly spread to other departments. It is accessible through any web browser, no passwords necessary. The tool is very useful when one wants to illustrate the concepts of competence and performance as conceived by Chomsky, how syntactic trees can be applied and, if time permits, what CFGs are. This exercise does require a bit more effort as many students are unfamiliar with formal language, but it is quite easy to make it fun since the freedom in defining the lexicon is limitless - something that has proven to be quite amusing.

Arongo, Arongo - why have you forsaken me?

Patrick Littell constructed a problem about the language on the island of Manam for NACLO in 2008. This problem deals with different ways of expressing location in space, turns out that the language of the island of Manam has a rather unusual system. The students are given a map of the island and some sentences in the language describing the location of certain houses on the map. This problem has been adapted into a small role playing game for the Lingolympiaden workshops.

The students are playing a group of field linguists who arrive to the island to study the indigenous language. There is only one person, Arongo, on the island with whom they have a common language (Tok Pisin). He was supposed to meet him when they arrived, but since they were late due to a storm he has returned to his home. They have to locate him by deciphering what the natives are saying to them, i.e. the sentences from the the original problem. They do not receive all sentences at once, they get them in small batches along with other clues (in step 2 they learn that there is a volcano). This gives them smaller amount of text to process at the same time, which makes it look less overwhelming. They also get to share their ideas and conclusions with each other and test their hypothesis on new data. Thus, learning how to approach a complex problem.

If there is plenty of time there is also the possibility of discussing other problems that field linguists might encounter.

5 Conclusions

The aim of the organisers and nature of the secondary school system determine the shape of the Olympiad of Linguistics in a specific country. In the case of Sweden the olympiad is primarily focused on reaching secondary school students with the message that linguistics is fun and they should pursue it further. An Olympiad more geared towards making students of natural sciences and programming interested in languages might look different (but not necessarily).

Lingolympiaden makes use of the expertise competence of the staff at the universities in the problem construction but also for lectures and teaching material, the universities use Lingolympiaden as a way of reaching potential students. YSS, the County Council of Stockholm and the Royal Academy of Letters support Lingolympiadens efforts to encourage the the youth of Sweden to be interested in social sciences and humanities in general and linguistics in particular. Teachers of modern languages and the new humanities programme use Lingolympiaden to improve their classes and provide extra-curricular activities for their students. And lastly: the students of secondary schools in Sweden use Lingolympiaden to try out what linguistics is all about and whether it is fun. It is their interest and their curiosity that is at the core of Lingolympiaden and other projects by YSS.

6 Future

As the contest grows there will hopefully be more opportunities to communicate with students and teachers of secondary schools and become more involved in their education. Lingolympiaden is a small contest aimed at providing an all-day outing at the university for secondary school students, but if there is interest there might be local contests at the schools themselves as well.

The Swedish government is right now considering whether or not to support Lingolympiaden in the same way that they support the Swedish Olympiad of Informatics, Lego Robot contest, Chemistry Olympiad etc. If they do, that will be a great leap towards acknowledgement of the value of social and human sciences alongside the natural sciences. Linguistics is an interdisciplinary scientific field that covers classical humanities, social and human sciences, natural sciences like neurology and biology, and computational disciplines. There is no reason why a Olympiad of Linguistics should be excluded from support of Olympiads of Science.

References

Giljarova, Ksenija. 2008. Problem for IOL 2008 in Slanchev Bryag. *Drehu & Cemuhî*. Available at: `http://www.ioling.org/problems/2008/i3/`

Jones, Trey. 2006. Speculative Grammarian, Vol CLI, No 2. *Lingdoku—Like Sudoku, But For Linguists*. L'École de SpecGram, Washington D.C.

Lager, Torbjörn. 2002. PSG Web Laboratory. Available at: `http://www.ling.gu.se/~lager/Labs/PSG-Lab/`

Litell, Patrick. 2008. Problem for NACLO 2008. *Manam, I'm Anam*. Available at: `http://www.naclo.cs.cmu.edu/assets/problems/naclo08r2.pdf`

Correspondence Seminar: Bringing Linguistics to High Schools

Matěj Korvas
Charles University in Prague
Faculty of Mathematics and Physics
Institute of Applied and Formal Linguistics
korvas@ufal.mff.cuni.cz

Vojtěch Diatka
Charles University in Prague
Faculty of Arts
Department of Linguistics
Vojta.Diatka@gmail.com

Abstract

We present the concept of a correspondence seminar as a way to complement and support one-time contests, especially olympiads. We evaluate specific payoffs of this way of teaching linguistics, and compare its nature to that of a linguistics olympiad. We believe that the correspondence seminar is a great way to introduce talented high school students to linguistics.

1 Introduction

At high schools in the Czech Republic, linguistics is taught only marginally or not at all. Students talented in linguistics thus tend to focus their talent on other areas, not even knowing what linguistics is like. We have struggled to change the state of affairs, and provide an alternative to the state system in delivering linguistic education to high school students.

Up until recently, we exposed the high school students to linguistics only through a correspondence seminar. By the term *correspondence seminar*, we mean a form of voluntary education where students and teachers exchange assignments and their solutions by postal correspondence (or more recently, via electronic communication in a similar way). This concept is described in more detail in Section 2. However, as IOL[1] (International Linguistics Olympiad; Radev et al. (2008)) came to our attention, we learned that despite the strong Czech linguistic tradition (Vachek and Dušková, 1983), there was no contest organised to select the Czech team for IOL. Hence we started the Czech Linguistic Olympiad (ČLO)[2] last year, and we have since observed some notable differences in the nature of the two formats, which we shall summarise in this paper.

We will start by giving a brief overview of the history of correspondence seminars, including Pralinka, the seminar in linguistics. In fact, correspondence seminar is not a new concept. The oldest contest based on postal correspondence, to our knowledge, is the Hungarian High School Mathematics and Physics Journal.[3] It dates back to as early as 1894, and with two interruptions, it survived up to the present. Thanks to the fact that it is translated into English, it is open to international audiences.

To the best of our knowledge, most correspondence seminars are organised in the area of former Czechoslovakia. The Slovak seminars include KMS[4] (mathematics), FKS[5] (physics), and STROM[6] (mathematics). The last mentioned one claims to have the longest tradition in the area of former Czechoslovakia, having been established in 1976. Correspondence seminars organised in the Czech Republic include MKS[7] (mathematics; founded 1981), FYKOS[8] (physics; 1986), and KSICHT[9] (chemistry; 2002; cf. Řezanka et al. (2012)). The seminars mentioned above have grown very popular – they commonly have several hundred participants each year.

Our correspondence seminar in linguistics is called Pralinka.[10] It was founded in 2008 and has about 14 participants each year, this low number being one significant difference to olympiads. During the five years, over 100 linguistic problems

[1] http://www.ioling.org

[2] http://lingol.cz

[3] http://www.komal.hu/info/bemutatkozas.e.shtml

[4] http://www.kms.sk

[5] http://fks.sk/english/english.php

[6] http://seminar.strom.sk/

[7] http://mks.mff.cuni.cz

[8] http://fykos.org/

[9] http://ksicht.natur.cuni.cz/o-ksichtu

[10] http://ufal.mff.cuni.cz/pralinka/english.php

have been created and published in Pralinka.

The contents and workings of the correspondence seminar are explained in detail in the following section. In Section 3, we point out differences between the correspondence seminar and an olympiad. In Section 4, we show sample problems created for Pralinka, and conclude with plans for the future in Section 5.

2 The Concept of a Correspondence Seminar

We will present the concept of a correspondence seminar on the concrete example of Pralinka. In Pralinka, we publish four issues featuring various linguistics problems each year. Students are supposed to solve as many problems as they can, and they have about six weeks to send us their solutions. We mark and comment on the solutions before sending them back to the participants. In a few weeks' time, a new issue is put together from new problem specifications and authors' solutions to previous problems. The specifications of the individual problems are linked together with a story, partly to provide motivation for the problems, partly to make the booklet more attractive for the reader.

The first issue is sent with other faculty propagation materials, including other correspondence seminars, in the printed form to high school teachers countrywide. This is the only occassion when Pralinka uses traditional post. Every issue is published on our web page as a PDF, and participants' solutions and their corrections are submitted to an integrated system again as document files. An appropriately formatted PDF of each issue is provided so that whoever is interested, can easily print out the booklet at their site. Apart from the system for collecting problem submissions and their corrections, another online interface of Pralinka is its Facebook page where every new issue is announced and participants can discuss with the organisers.

An essential motivation for the participants are points we give them for their solutions. Seminars with a higher number of participants use the ranking of participants to select the ones eligible for the seminar summer school. Pralinka also has a short summer school each year, but we have no need to cut the number of its participants. Still, we reward the best ranking ones for their efforts with a prize.

Problems we publish in Pralinka can be divided into three classes: single problems, thematic problems and running tasks. *Single problems* are one-off tasks that typically include little or no theory. They usually require the students to discover a pattern in the provided linguistic data, or expand on a given topic.

Thematic problems form a completely different genre. Their constitutive feature is that they go deep into the topic. Every year, a different topic is chosen to be investigated by the students under the supervision of the organisers. Theory for the topic is extended in each issue of the seminar, and a very open formulation of a problem to solve is given. The problem specification in the next issue is largely determined by the students' contributions. Students are thus introduced to the selected branch of linguistics step by step, both theoretically and practically. Thematic problems in the history of Pralinka examined topics like meaning of words in context or verbal aspects and their use.

Lastly, *running tasks* or *series* are similar to thematic problems in many respects. They are on a selected topic each year, and gradually build up the theory. In contrast to thematic problems, assignments in each instance of the running task are precisely specified and solvers' answers do not influence the future direction of the series. Some running tasks explore phenomena from different layers of linguistic description using an artificial language as the subject, others have the form of a textbook text split into chapters, providing exercises for each chapter. The latter kind covered topics such as language universals, Arabic (an introduction to the language) or semantics.

An important feature of the correspondence seminar is the individual attitude to students and their solutions. Correcting solutions does not consist only of assigning the appropriate number of points. More important is the feedback in the form of advice and questions related to the contestant's own text.

3 Comparison to Olympiads

We now turn to the comparison of a correspondence seminar and an olympiad as two alternative ways of promoting linguistics among gifted high school students. We will discuss the following aspects: time required for solving the problems, nature of the problems, attitude to linguistic knowledge, use of external information sources, and at-

type	Plka 10/11	Plka 12/13	ČLO 12/13
total	22 (100%)	18 (100%)	14 (100%)
seg+al	5 (23%)	7 (39%)	11 (79%)
theory	15 (68%)	7 (39%)	0 (0%)
open	16 (73%)	10 (56%)	4 (29%)

Table 1: Types of tasks in a sample from ČLO and Pralinka

type	Plka 10/11	Plka 12/13	ČLO 12/13
total	114 (100%)	119 (100%)	2393 (100%)
seg+al	23 (20%)	55 (46%)	2268 (95%)
theory	58 (51%)	43 (36%)	0 (0%)
open	86 (75%)	79 (66%)	665 (28%)

Table 2: Number of students that attempted solving different types of problems in a sample from ČLO and Pralinka

tractiveness to students.

Linguistic olympiads are generally one-time events whose participants are given just a few hours to solve a number of problems. They are thus motivated to quickly discover just as many features of the problem as needed to find answers for the questions posed. It is likely that solving such a problem involves just the short term memory, and the related ideas are much easier to forget. In contrast, participants of a correspondence seminar have lots of time to think each problem over, therefore, firstly, the problems need to provide enough food for thought, and secondly, this leads the solvers to internalise the ideas behind the problem much better.

For typically large numbers of participants of olympiads, especially in school rounds, olympiads need to have a clear grading scheme, hence closed-ended questions are the best suited. In contrast, problems in a correspondence seminar can be (and, in Pralinka, they often are) open-ended. This again supports deeper thinking about the problem.

The different composition of Pralinka versus ČLO in terms of problem types is quantified in Table 1. We counted problems from the 2010/2011 (the last school year before we launched ČLO) and 2012/2013 (this year; one issue could not yet be included) editions of Pralinka and this year's ČLO. We assessed for each problem whether:

1. it is solved by applying the common pattern of establishing a segmentation of the linguistic data (e.g. words into morphemes, Chinese characters into two parts) and then aligning the corresponding segments (row "seg+al" in the table);
2. theory is explained as part of the problem ("theory");
3. an open-ended question is posed ("open").

Table 2 follows the same layout but lists counts of students that attempted to solve each problem.[11] The numbers justify our claim that problems in Pralinka are more often open-ended than those in the olympiad. They also show that there is much more space for presenting theory as part of the problems in Pralinka, which we expand on in the following paragraph. Another fact illustrated by the numbers is that we adjusted Pralinka problems to be more similar to olympiad problems when ČLO was founded, in order to prepare Pralinka solvers for the olympiad. Lastly, the difference in the number of attempted solutions between Pralinka and ČLO is huge, as evident from Table 2. We try to explain this fact in the paragraphs below.

Another important difference regards the amount of linguistic knowledge presented *together with* the problems and required to solve them. The olympiad is primarily concerned with testing the contestant's skills in analysing an unknown language, often their analytical thinking in general. On the other hand, the correspondence seminar puts stress on teaching not only skills, but also knowledge, in order to widen contestants' horizons. To this end, problems published in Pralinka often comprise two parts: a theoretical one and a practical one, the latter part helping the solver practise immediately what was expounded in the former part.

The two formats differ also with respect to the approach to various *external sources* of knowledge. Olympiads strictly forbid using them, whereas in the correspondence seminar, their use is welcome. O. Šteffl, a prominent Czech education specialist, claims that "...the accessibility of information has dramatically changed. If I type 'coelenterate' into Google, what appears in a few seconds are BBC documentaries, pictures, explanations, curiosities, and I can search for context and links in this topic."[12] Situation is the same for linguistic knowledge. There is a vast amount of

[11] Entries in Table 2 are measured in student-problems.

[12] source (original in Czech): `respekt.ihned.cz/c1-55775590-jsme-posedli-selekci-deti`

linguistic information accessible on the Internet. In Pralinka, even though we usually aim to create problems that cannot be simply solved by consulting Wikipedia or other sources, we are pleased to hear when our participants bother to use online resources, or even borrow a grammar book of a language in order to understand the topic more deeply, as provoking students to study on their own is one of our goals.

Finally, it is remarkable how few students get involved in the correspondence seminar, compared to the olympiad. The olympiad started only last year and it already has an order of magnitude more participants. This can be attributed to a simple fact that general awareness of linguistics as an interesting discipline among Czech high school students is very poor compared to mathematics or physics. Students thus do not show active interest in linguistics, although they get involved once their teachers give them linguistic problems at school during the olympiad school round.

We believe that participants of Pralinka are generally more interested in linguistics than participants of ČLO, and hence are more likely to enroll in a linguistics study programme at the university and be successful in it. Unfortunately, data we could use to test this hypothesis is not collected yet, although currently there is an effort of the Faculty of Mathematics and Physics to quantify the effectivity of its propagation activities including Pralinka.

4 Sample Problems

In this section, we present two examples of problems that appeared in Pralinka, which we think are particularly suitable for a correspondence seminar.

4.1 Labovian cups

In this problem, we motivate the participants to replicate Labov's famous experiment with tableware (Labov, 1973). General introduction to the topic of categories which do not have clear-cut boundaries is given through a simple dialogue led by two characters, rather than a technical exposition. Participants are then presented with tasks connected to two pictures of tableware (see Figure 1).

Tasks were as follows:

(a) (b)

Figure 1: Labov's tableware experiment in Pralinka

1. Do you think that the content of a container would influence whether it is called *cup*, *bowl*, or *vase*? We could fill it with flowers, tea or mashed potatoes.

2. Do your own experiment. Print out the pictures (those shown in Figure 1) and ask at least three people to name the objects. Show them first the container without contents, and then the same container with contents. Make sure that you show only one container at a time. Instruction could be that simple: "Tell me what you see." Write down the answers and expand on them.

4.2 Word alignment

In this problem, we present the concept of word alignment as used in machine translation (Koehn, 2007, pp. 113–124), and ask the students to elaborate on possible configurations in word alignment tables.

The task is motivated by the main character of Pralinka constructing a dictionary, trying to capture all translation options for every phrase.

This problem is clearly not suitable for olympiads, whereas it fits nicely the format of a correspondence seminar. Let us now comment on how well some students can cope with such problems, using two quite different kinds of analysis.

One participant performed a principled analysis of the possible configurations of alignment points, distinguishing cases with a single alignment point in the row and column, multiple points in a row or column, and multiple points in the same row *and* column. He illustrates his classification using examples including those shown in Figure 2. The first two examples in Figure 2 (the first one meaning "my country") are based on

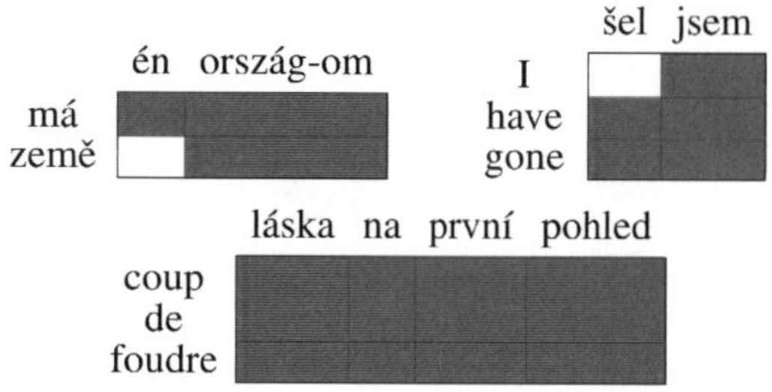

Figure 2: Examples of alignments from Solver 1

different ways grammatical categories are marked in different languages, including the first person and possessive markers in the first example, and first person and the tense in the second example. The third example ("love at first sight") shows two phrases that are translation of each other but cannot be analysed into smaller units that would also translate one to the other.

Another participant focuses in her solution on the most interesting cases, showing typical properties of different languages, such as the tendency towards analytic or synthetic forms, and different word order. Even though she does not come up with a classification system, she gives a comprehensive overview of particular interesting examples. A few of her alignment examples are shown in Figure 3. The first example again demonstrates

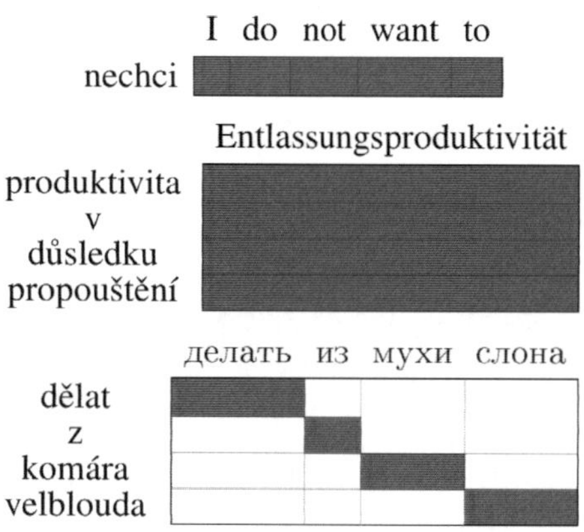

Figure 3: Examples of alignments from Solver 2

(a more extreme) difference in expressing grammatical categories in a flective (Czech) and an isolating (English) language. The second example ("productivity resulting from layoffs") illustrates the same meaning being expressed using multiple words in Czech, as compared to the synthetic German. The last example ("make a mountain out of a molehill") is parallel to the example with *coup de foudre*, but the phrases decompose in this case, even though they result in the *mosquito–mouse* and *camel–elephant* translation pairs.

5 Future Work

It is our ambition to make Pralinka international, either by organising the summer school jointly for Czech and foreign students, or by translating our problems into English and inviting foreign students to solve them. However, the latter could meet with a larger response than the existing organising team can handle, thus we greatly welcome any helpers before that transition is made, both to participate in the organisation, and help in promoting the seminar.

Acknowledgments

We thank Lěra Ivanova and Adam Pospíšil for the consent to cite their problem solutions, and Ondřej Dušek, Lukáš Žilka and the anonymous reviewers for their corrections and helpful comments. Pralinka has been supported by the Faculty of Mathematics and Physics of the Charles University, ČLO has been supported jointly by the Faculty of Mathematics and Physics and the Faculty of Arts of the Charles University.

References

Philipp Koehn. 2007. *Statistical Machine Translation*. Univ. Pr., Cambridge.

William Labov. 1973. The boundaries of words and their meanings. In Bailey and R. W. Shuy, editors, *New Ways of analyzing variation in English*, pages 340–373. Washington, D.C.: Georgetown University Press.

Dragomir R. Radev, Lori S. Levin, and Thomas E. Payne. 2008. The North American Computational Linguistics Olympiad (NACLO). In *Proceedings of the Third Workshop on Issues in Teaching Computational Linguistics*, TeachCL '08, pages 87–96, Stroudsburg, PA, USA. Association for Computational Linguistics.

Michal Řezanka, Pavel Řezanka, Luděk Míka, Pavla Perlíková, and Karel Berka. 2012. Korespondenční seminář inspirovaný chemickou tematikou (KSICHT) [Correspondence seminar inspired by chemistry topics (KSICHT)]. In *Chemické listy*, volume 106, page 319–322, Prague, Czech Republic, April.

Josef Vachek and Libuše Dušková. 1983. *Praguiana: some basic and less known aspects of the Prague Linguistic School*. Number v. 12 in Linguistic & literary studies in Eastern Europe (LLSEE). J.Benjamins, Amsterdam ; Philadelphia.

Artificial IntelliDance: Teaching Machine Learning through a Choreography

Apoorv Agarwal
Department of Computer Science
Columbia University, New York, USA
apoorv@cs.columbia.edu

Caitlin Trainor
Department of Dance
Barnard College, Columbia University
caitlinmarytrainor@gmail.com

Abstract

In this paper we present a choreography that explains the process of supervised machine learning. We present how a perceptron (in its dual form) uses convolution kernels to learn to differentiate between two categories of *objects*. Convolution kernels such as string kernels and tree kernels are widely used in Natural Language Processing (NLP) applications. However, the baggage associated with learning the theory behind convolution kernels, which extends beyond graduate linear algebra, makes the adoption of this technology intrinsically difficult. The main challenge in creating this choreography was that we were required to represent these mathematical equations at their *meaning* level before we could translate them into the language of movement. By orchestrating such a choreography, we believe, we have obviated the need for people to posses advanced math background in order to appreciate the core ideas of using convolution kernels in a supervised learning setting.

1 Introduction

Natural Language Processing (NLP) and Machine Learning (ML) are making a significant impact in our day to day lives. Advancement in these areas of research is changing the way humans interact with each other and with objects around them. For example, speech to speech translation is making it possible for people speaking different languages to communicate seamlessly.[1] In this eco-system, where machines and objects around us are becoming smarter, there is a need to make this complex technology available to a general audience.

The Dance Your PhD competition[2] is a recent effort that encourages doctoral students pursuing research in Physics, Chemistry, Biology and Social Sciences to explain the scientific ideas in their theses through movement. The main advantage of this approach is that the scientific ideas become available to a general audience through a medium that is both visual and entertaining. The main challenge, of course, is to abstract away from the technical vocabulary and physicalize these scientific ideas.

In this paper, we present a choreography that explains the process of learning from data in a supervised setting. Through this choreography, we bring out some of the main ideas of supervised machine learning, including representing data as structured objects and formulating similarity functions that a machine uses to calculate distances between data points. While these are general ideas, more relevant to an audience that is not familiar with machine learning, the choreography may also be used for explaining convolution kernels to researchers familiar with machine learning but not necessarily familiar with how a perceptron uses a convolution kernel in its dual form.

The main challenge in creating this choreography was that we were required to represent these mathematical equations at the *meaning* level before translating them into the language of movement. In doing so, our primary concerns were accuracy, aesthetics, and legibility. The scientific ideas at hand could not be compromised, and yet a literal representation of the symbols would negate the intent of the project.

[1] http://www.bbn.com/technology/speech/speech_to_speech_translation

[2] http://gonzolabs.org/dance/

Equally vital to the success of the piece is the quality of the choreography on its own formal and aesthetic terms. The challenge of the translation was both critical to the process and also enriching, because it deepened our understanding of convolution kernels.

As Jason Eisner correctly notes in his paper on interactive spreadsheets for teaching the forward-backward algorithm (Eisner, 2002) – *They are concrete, visual, playful, sometimes interactive, and remain available to the students after the lecture ends* – we believe this choreography shares the same spirit. Artificial IntelliDance functions to explain a relatively sophisticated machine learning paradigm in an accessible and entertaining format that can be viewed repeatedly.[3]

The rest of the paper is structured as follows: In section 2, we review the perceptron algorithm, its dual form and convolution kernels. In section 3 we present details of the choreography, focusing on the aspects that explain the process of supervised machine learning and bring out the strengths and weaknesses of kernel learning. We conclude in Section 4.

2 The Perceptron algorithm and Convolution Kernels

The perceptron algorithm is an online learning algorithm invented by Frank Rosenblatt in 1958 (Rosenblatt, 1958). Given a set of training data points, $D = \{(\mathbf{x_i}, y_i)\}$, where $y_i \in \{1, -1\}$, the algorithm works as follows:[4]

1. Start with the all-zeroes weight vector $\mathbf{w_1} = 0$, and initialize t to 1.

2. Given $\mathbf{x_i}$, predict positive if $\mathbf{w_t} \cdot \mathbf{x_i} > 0$

3. On a mistake, update as follows:

   $\mathbf{w_{t+1}} \leftarrow \mathbf{w_t} + y_i\mathbf{x_i}$

4. $t \leftarrow t + 1$

In natural language, a perceptron maintains a weight vector $\mathbf{w_t}$ at time instance t. The weight vector is initialized to zero at the start of the algorithm. The perceptron receives one data point after the other. For each data point, it predicts the category of the data point by calculating its dot product with the weight vector. If the dot product is greater than zero, it predicts the category of the data point as 1, and -1 otherwise. On a mistake, the perceptron updates the weight vector by adding the product of the data point ($\mathbf{x_i}$) and its category (1 or -1).

The key idea here is that the weight vector is a linear combination of the training data points whose categories the perceptron predicted incorrectly at the time of training. The algorithm *remembers* these incorrectly classified data points by *marking* them with their true category (1 or -1). Abusing terminology, we refer to these incorrectly classified training data points as support vectors. Notationally, the final weight vector then is $\mathbf{w} = \sum_{k=1}^{N_s} y_k \mathbf{x_k}$, where N_s is the number of support vectors.

This simple fact that the weight vector is a linear combination of the data points has a deeper consequence – to predict the category of an unseen example, call it $\mathbf{x}$, all we need is a dot product of $\mathbf{x}$ with all the support vectors: $\mathbf{w} \cdot \mathbf{x} = \sum_{k=1}^{N_s} y_k(\mathbf{x_k} \cdot \mathbf{x})$. This is usually referred to as the dual form of the perceptron. The dual form allows for the use of kernels because the dot product between two examples can be replaced by a kernel as follows: $\mathbf{w} \cdot \mathbf{x} = \sum_{k=1}^{N_s} y_k K(\mathbf{x_k}, \mathbf{x})$. This is exactly where convolution kernels come into the picture. We review those next.

Convolution kernels, first introduced by David Haussler (1999), can be viewed as functions that calculate similarities between abstract objects, $K : X \times X \rightarrow \mathbb{R}$, where X is the set of abstract objects. Since their introduction, convolution kernels have been widely used in many NLP applications (Collins and Duffy, 2002; Lodhi et al., 2002; Zelenko et al., 2003; Culotta and Sorensen, 2004; Moschitti, 2004; Zhou et al., 2007; Moschitti et al., 2008; Agarwal and Rambow, 2010; Agarwal et al., 2011). The reason for their popular use in NLP applications is that text has *natural* representations such as strings, trees, and graphs. Representing text in its natural representation alleviates the need for fine-grained feature engineering and is therefore a convenient way of data representation. Using this natural data representation, convolution kernels calculate

[3]The video is available at the following URL: http://tinyurl.com/mte8wda

[4]From lecture notes of Avrim Blum: http://www.cs.cmu.edu/~avrim/ML09/lect0126.pdf. Modified for our purposes.

the similarity between two objects by recursively dividing the objects into "parts", calculating the similarity between smaller parts, and aggregating these similarities to report a similarity between objects. For example, the way a string kernel will calculate the similarity between two strings (say "abc" and "aec") is by mapping each string into an *implicit* feature space and then calculating the similarity between the two strings by taking a dot product of the mappings (see Table 1). The feature space is called *implicit* because the kernel never explicitly writes out these features (or sub-structures). It calculates the similarity by using a dynamic program that recurses over these structures to find similar sub-structures.

	a	b	c	e	ab	ac	bc	ae	ec
"abc"	1	1	1	0	1	1	1	0	0
"aec"	1	0	1	1	0	1	0	1	1
$\vec{v}$	1	0	1	0	0	1	0	0	0

Table 1: An example showing how a string kernel will calculate the similarity between two strings. The implicit feature space is {a, b, c, e, ab, ac, bc, ae, ec }. $\vec{v}$ refers to the dot product of the vectors of the two strings. Similarity between these two strings is $\sum_{i=1}^{9} v_i = 3$

Thus, convolution kernels allow the learner to make similarity calculations without compromising the original structure of the objects (unlike feature engineering, where every object is represented as a vector in a finite dimensional space, thus losing the original structure of objects). This was the key observation that lead us to define *objects* as dance forms, and to our choice of using convolution kernels for explaining the machine learning process through a choreography. We discuss this in detail in the next section.

3 Artificial IntelliDance

In 2011, we created a choreography to present the idea of how a machine goes through the process of learning from data. We presented a perceptron, in its dual form, that uses convolution kernels to learn how to differentiate between two categories of *objects*. The 15 minute choreography is supported by a narrative, which is an interaction between a machine, depicted by a dancer, and a *user*, whose voice is heard but who remains unseen.

One of the main and early challenges we ran into during the ideation of the choreography had to do with the definition of *objects*. Though the central goal of the choreography was to explain a scientific idea, we wanted the choreography to maintain its aesthetic value. As a consequence of this constraint, we decided to stay away from defining objects as *things* that would restrict the dancers from moving freely in a natural way.

As discussed in the previous section, since convolution kernels allow for a natural representation of objects, we define our objects to be two dance forms: Ballet and Modern dance. Much like string kernels, where the implicit feature space is the space of sub-strings (that form a string), in our case, the high dimensional kernel space is the space of sub-movements (that form a movement). Each dancer is a data point, seen as a sequence of movements in an infinite dimensional space.

Figure 1: Above is a scene from one of the performances in which the machine, represented by the dancer in silver, "considers" the data. Prominently featured are data point dancers in red and yellow, both of whom have been marked with category-differentiating shapes (round for Ballet and diamond for Modern).

The choreography is broken into multiple phases. In the first phase, we motivate the need for machine learning, or pattern recognition, by presenting an apparently chaotic scene; all of the dancers are onstage at once, performing unique movement sequences, with only brief moments of synchronized action. The cacophonous dancing conveys the overwhelming difficulty for data scientists to find patterns in data using the naked eye. The dialogue advances the choreography to the next phase, where we sketch out the learning process.

In the learning phase, the machine starts by making a prediction on the first data point. Since the machine has no prior knowledge ($\mathbf{w_1} = 0$), it makes a random prediction and gets the category wrong. The machine marks the dancer with a symbol in order to remember the data point ($\mathbf{w_t} \leftarrow \mathbf{w_t} + y_i\mathbf{x_i}$). The machine is then asked to make a prediction on a second data point. The machine compares this new data point with the data point it marked and makes a prediction ($\mathbf{w} \cdot \mathbf{x} = \sum_{k=1}^{N_s} y_k K(\mathbf{x_k}, \mathbf{x})$). Once again, it gets the category wrong and marks the second data point as well. This process continues until the machine has seen all the training instances and has selected data points it *thinks* encode structures important for classification.

Marking of dancers is done explicitly where the machine dancer attaches a round or triangular symbol to the data points: round is for Ballet and triangle is for Modern (see Figure 1). This is analogous to how a perceptron attaches positive and negative weights to the data points belonging to positive and negative categories respectively.

The narration points out a big limitation of convolution kernel methods, which is, in the worst case, every data-point is compared with every other data point in the training data, thus making the learning process slow (because the machine needs to go through the training data twice).

We also differentiate between the low dimensional feature space, in which the machine is unable to separate the data, and the high dimensional space, which offers distinguishability. The set of inactive training data points, i.e. the data points in a low dimensional feature space, is depicted by a clump of dancers in a corner who are hardly moving. The set of data points that are actively moving lie in a high dimensional feature space in which the machine learns a linear separator.

The next phase is testing, in which the machine compares the test dancers with the dancers it marked in the learning phase. After comparing each test point with all the support vectors, the machine makes a prediction. This phase concludes by showing that the machine has in fact learned to differentiate between the two categories.

The user is impressed and asks the machine to reveal the secret sauce. In this part of the choreography we visually describe how convolution kernels go about calculating similarities between two abstract objects, by breaking the object into parts, and recursing over the parts to calculate similarity. This action is illustrated by a comparison of similar movements and sub-movements as executed by a ballet and modern dancer. Situated side by side, the two dancers fragment the movements into increasingly smaller bits so as to make differences in the two forms of dance (objects) more visibly comparable. We also highlight the reason for the machine to look at a pair of data points instead of individual data points. The reason is that the machine does not remember the sub-structures important for classification (because the implicit feature space is enormous). By marking the data points, it only remembers the data points that encode these sub-structures. To this, the user voice points out another limitation of using convolution kernels; interpretability of models is hard. We can learn predictive models, but the fine grained structures important for classification remain hidden.

The piece ends with all the dancers linearly separated into categories in a high dimensional implicit feature space. Through the narration we point out the main differences and similarities between the two forms of dance, which are aesthetically visible but are sometimes hard to articulate.

4 Conclusion

In this paper, we presented a choreography that illustrates the process of supervised machine learning using a perceptron and convolution kernels. The choreography is structured around a scene in which the machine (represented by a dancer) learns to differentiate between two categories of objects, ballet and modern dance. The choreography not only explains the process of machine learning and how convolution kernels work, it also brings out two major limitations of using convolution kernels visually – having to go through the data twice, which makes the learning process slow, and that the interpretability of the models is hard, because the important substructures are not stored explicitly. While the general ideas about supervised machine learning may be more relevant to an audience that is not familiar with machine learning, the choreography may also be used to explain convolution kernels (in a visual and entertaining way) to researchers familiar with machine learning but not necessarily familiar with how a perceptron uses a convolution kernel in its dual form.

Artificial IntelliDance premiered at Barnard College in April 2012, and has since been invited to perform at the World Science Festival 2012 and TEDx ColumbiaEngineering 2012. The audience was comprised of a combination of scientists and non-scientists, including dance artists, undergraduate and graduate students, and the general public. The primary concepts of the presentation were understood clearly by a number of viewers lacking familiarity with any machine learning paradigm as evidenced by the post-presentation discussions. Unfortunately, we do not have a more precise evaluation as to how many people actually understood the scientific ideas. The only "evaluation" we have is that the video continues to be showcased; we were recently invited to showcase it at Australia's National Science Week 2013. However, we have not yet heard of the video being used in a Machine Learning lecture.

In addition to functioning as an educational tool, a noteworthy outcome of the project is that it fosters dialogue between the general public and the arts and computer science communities.

Acknowledgments

We would like to thank Caronae Howell, Kapil Thadani, and anonymous reviewers for useful comments. We thank the dancers involved in the production and performance of the piece (in no particular order): Aditi Dhruv, Jenna Simon, Morgan Caglianone, Maddie James, Claire Salant, Anna Brown Massey, Emily Craver, Mindy Upin, Temple Kemezis, Taylor Gordon, Chelsea Cusack, Lane Halperin, Lisa Fitzgerald and Eleanor Barisser. We would like to thank Robert Boston for music and Marlon Cherry for voice of the user.

References

Apoorv Agarwal and Owen Rambow. 2010. Automatic detection and classification of social events. In *Proceedings of the 2010 Conference on Empirical Methods in Natural Language Processing*, pages 1024–1034, Cambridge, MA, October. Association for Computational Linguistics.

Apoorv Agarwal, Boyi Xie, Ilia Vovsha, Owen Rambow, and Rebecca Passonneau. 2011. Sentiment analysis of twitter data. In *Proceedings of the Workshop on Language in Social Media (LSM 2011)*, pages 30–38, Portland, Oregon, June. Association for Computational Linguistics.

Michael Collins and Nigel Duffy. 2002. New ranking algorithms for parsing and tagging: Kernels over discrete structures, and the voted perceptron. In *Proceedings of the 40th annual meeting on association for computational linguistics*, pages 263–270. Association for Computational Linguistics.

Aron Culotta and Jeffrey Sorensen. 2004. Dependency tree kernels for relation extraction. In *Proceedings of the 42nd Meeting of the Association for Computational Linguistics (ACL'04), Main Volume*, pages 423–429, Barcelona, Spain, July.

Jason Eisner. 2002. An interactive spreadsheet for teaching the forward-backward algorithm. In *Proceedings of the ACL-02 Workshop on Effective Tools and Methodologies for Teaching Natural Language Processing and Computational Linguistics*, pages 10–18, Philadelphia, Pennsylvania, USA, July. Association for Computational Linguistics.

David Haussler. 1999. Convolution kernels on discrete structures. Technical report, University of California at Santa Cruz.

Huma Lodhi, Craig Saunders, John Shawe-Taylor, Nello Christianini, and Chris Watkins. 2002. Text classification using string kernels. *The Journal of Machine Learning Research*, 2:419–444.

Alessandro Moschitti, Daniele Pighin, and Roberto Basili. 2008. Tree kernels for semantic role labeling. *Special Issue on Semantic Role Labeling, Computational Linguistics Journal,*.

Alessandro Moschitti. 2004. A study on convolution kernels for shallow semantic parsing. In *Proceedings of the 42nd Conference on Association for Computational Linguistic*.

Frank Rosenblatt. 1958. The perceptron. *Psych. Rev*, 65(6):386–408.

Dmitry Zelenko, Chinatsu Aone, and Anthony Richardella. 2003. Kernel methods for relation extraction. *The Journal of Machine Learning Research*, 3:1083–1106.

GuoDong Zhou, Min Zhang, DongHong Ji, and QiaoMing Zhu. 2007. Tree kernel-based relation extraction with context-sensitive structured parse tree information. In *Proceedings of EMNLP-CoNLL*.

Treebanking for Data-driven Research in the Classroom

John Lee, Ying Cheuk Hui, Yin Hei Kong
Halliday Centre for Intelligent Applications of Language Studies
Department of Chinese, Translation and Linguistics
City University of Hong Kong
{jsylee,yingchui,yhkong}@cityu.edu.hk

Abstract

Data-driven research in linguistics typically involves the processes of data annotation, data visualization and identification of relevant patterns. We describe our experience in incorporating these processes at an undergraduate course on language information technology. Students collectively annotated the syntactic structures of a set of Classical Chinese poems; the resulting treebank was put on a platform for corpus search and visualization; finally, using this platform, students investigated research questions about the text of the treebank.

1 Introduction

Treebanks are now increasingly used as pedagogical tools (Crane et al., 2012), chiefly in two ways. On the one hand, in linguistics courses, students may use existing treebanks to perform quantitative analysis on syntactic patterns. On the other, in language courses, students may annotate syntactic structures to reinforce grammatical concepts, creating new treebanks. In this paper, we describe our experience in integrating these two processes into a research project in an undergraduate course, and discuss its benefits and challenges.

The project formed part of a course entitled "Language Information Technology". With no previous training, students collectively annotated the dependency structures of a portion of the *Three Hundred Tang Poems*, a popular anthology of Classical Chinese poems. The instructor edited the annotations, compiled them into a dependency treebank, and made it available for search and visualization on a web-based interface. Then, in a research assignment, students tackled questions on Chinese poetry with this treebank, which they had created with their own hands.

Combining the creation of a treebank with its use in a research assignment has many benefits. With respect to pedagogy, the assignment demonstrates to students the practical rationale for treebanks; the treebanking exercise familiarized students with the data and annotation scheme, helping them perform better on the assignment. With respect to longer-term effects, students perceive their own, tangible contribution to a field of scholarly research, in the form of linguistic annotations that are reusable by other scholars. The hands-on practice of a novel research methodology --- data-driven study in linguistics and literature --- should encourage them to apply it in their future fields of study.

The rest of the paper is organized as follows. Section 2 outlines previous use of treebanks in the classroom. Section 3 describes how our course was structured. Section 4 explains how students created the treebank, which formed the basis of the research assignment discussed in section 5. Section 6 presents the lessons learned and concludes.

2 Previous Work

Many current systems support the use of linguistic corpora for teaching and learning. One of many examples, the Visual Interactive Syntax Learning (VISL) system allows students to search, view, construct and label parse trees (Bick, 2005). The GATE system similarly facilitates corpus annotation, but it can also perform a variety of NLP tasks including POS tagging and parsing (Bontcheva et al., 2002).

These systems facilitate pedagogical use of treebanks in two main ways. First, students visualize parse trees and search for linguistic structures on existing treebanks. These functions support empirical and quantitative analysis of linguistic phenomena. Second, students also use their editing environment to create new dependency annotations on text, as exercises in learning a new language. The resulting treebank can then be made available for all scholars.

The latter type of usage has been implemented in Classics courses at six American universities. Students made dependency annotations on a Latin or Greek text, which the instructor then reconciled. The results contributed to the Latin and Ancient Greek Dependency Treebanks that are being compiled at the Perseus Project. In a study on 13 students, who had received limited training, the inter-annotator accuracy averaged 54.5% (Bamman & Crane, 2010).

Treebanking itself has also been taught in a course (Volk et al., 2005). Another notable case where students collectively created new linguistic resources has been reported at a graduate course in multilingual grammar engineering (Bender, 2007). Each student developed a grammar for automatic parsing of a new language. Over time, students' work was found to be effective in bringing feedback to the core grammar, and to facilitate empirical research on cross-linguistic comparisons.

A significant novelty in our course design is that, after students create new annotations for a treebank, they share the data with the rest of the class, and apply the freshly compiled treebank for linguistic research. We now describe how these two processes were implemented.

3 Course Structure

The project described in this paper was integrated into "Language Information Technology", an undergraduate course offered at the Department of Chinese, Translation and Linguistics at City University of Hong Kong. In the past semester, 44 students were enrolled. All majored in the Chinese language. As can be expected in a humanities department, the students had no technical background or experience in natural language processing. While some had previously taken linguistics courses, none was familiar with dependency grammar or its annotation scheme.

The course lasted for 13 weeks; weekly meetings consisted of a one-hour lecture and a two-hour tutorial or practicum. Roughly one half of this course was devoted to the treebanking project. In the first week, part-of-speech (POS) tagging was introduced, with English as the example language. During the practicum, students reviewed POS concepts with exercises and Stanford's online tagger[1]. In the second, dependency trees were introduced, again using examples in English. Lectures in the third and fourth weeks turned the attention to Chinese POS and dependency trees, using respectively the schemes defined at the Penn Chinese Treebank (Xue et al., 2005) and Stanford (Chang et al., 2009). During the practicums, adaptations to these schemes for Classical Chinese (Lee, 2012; Lee & Kong, 2012) were presented. In the fifth week, the web interface for searching and visualizing treebanks, which would later be used for a research assignment (see section 5), was demonstrated. Also, students were assigned individual texts for POS tagging and dependency labeling (see section 4). The practicum was devoted to discussions on difficulties in annotation.

The annotations were due two weeks later. After editing by the instructor, the treebank was posted on the aforementioned web interface, and the assignment was released. Overall, each student received 15 hours of class time in preparation for the treebanking project.

4 Treebank Annotation

The first task of the students, described in this section, is to annotate dependency structures of a set of Classical Chinese texts. The newly created treebank would then be used in a second task, to be discussed in the next section.

4.1 Choice of Material

Among the various literary genres, poetry enjoys perhaps the most elevated status in the Classical Chinese tradition. 320 poems from the Tang Dynasty, considered the golden age for poetry, have been grouped together in an anthology referred to as the *Three Hundred Tang Poems*. This anthology is perhaps the most well-known in the canon of Classical Chinese literature, and is featured without exception in the Chinese curriculum in secondary schools.

For the treebanking project, this corpus is ideal because it is both non-toy and not prohibitively difficult. As well-known literary heritage, this corpus lends interesting and significant questions to the research assignment (section 5). Moreover, unlike many other Chinese Classics, these poems are relatively simple to analyze, with each line containing not more than 7 characters. All students can be expected to have previous expo-

[1] http://nlp.stanford.edu:8080/parser/

sure to some of the poems. Finally, since the text is of such central importance, the resulting treebank is likely to be relevant to other scholars. It is especially motivating for students that their efforts would have an impact long after they receive their grades for the course.

4.2 Annotation Set-up and Results

Each of the 44 students was assigned four different poems from the *Three Hundred Tang Poems* for annotation, with a total of 144 characters.

The instructor manually corrected the student annotations. Using the corrected version as gold standard, the students achieved 68.1% labeled attachment score (LAS)[2]. The quality of individual students' annotations varied widely, from the lowest LAS at less than 10%, to the top student who scored more than 95%. Students were allowed to discuss their annotations with the instructor, but the correct annotations were never disclosed to them.

Part-of-speech tagging. The students achieved 93.9% accuracy for POS tagging, which compares reasonably with the agreement rate of 95.1% among two annotators reported on similar texts in (Lee, 2012). The tags with the highest error rates are shown in Table 1. The most frequent pairs of confusion are among the tags VA (predicative adjectives), AD (adverbs), and JJ (attributive adjectives).

The lack of morphology in Classical Chinese likely contributed to the confusion between AD and JJ. Consider the phrase 閒/AD *xian* 'relaxed' 坐/VV *zuo* 'sit', the first two characters from the line 閒坐說玄宗 "while sitting relaxedly, [we] gossip about Emperor Xuan". Here, the word *xian* 'relaxed' is an adverb describing the manner of *zuo* 'sit'; however, the same form can also serves as an adjective, perhaps leading a student to tag it as JJ.

Even more frequent is the confusion between JJ and VA. A typical example is the phrase 燭/NN *zhu* 'candle' 影/NN *ying* 'shadow' 深/VA *shen* 'becomes dark', the last three characters in the line 雲母屏風燭影深 "the shadow of the candle on the mica screen becomes dark". Despite hints from the word order, the student mistakenly considered *shen* 'becomes dark' as an attributive, rather than predicative, adjective.

[2] As a comparison, two heavily trained annotators achieved 91.2% agreement on similar texts (Lee and Kong, 2012), and performance of automatic parsers can reach LAS at 75.6% (Lee and Wong, 2012).

Tag	Error rate	Tag	Error rate
AD	20.1%	M	13.8%
P	20.0%	LC	9.4%
VA	19.1%	CD	6.6%
VC	16.1%	JJ	4.4%
PN	11.9%		

Table 1. POS tags with the highest error rates.

Head selection. Among those characters whose POS tags are correctly labeled, head selection is correct 81.8% of the time. As shown in Table 2, among the various POS, students most frequently had difficulty selecting heads for verbs. While there was a wide range of different kinds of mistakes, the most common one is to mistakenly take a noun as head, using the dependency label vmod (verb modifier).

Series of adverbs (AD) also turned out to be problematic; a third of the errors with AD fell into this case. Consider the two adverbs *bu* and *fu* in the phrase 不/AD *bu* 'not' 復/AD *fu* 'again' 返/VV *fan* 'return', the last three characters in the line 黃鶴一去不返 "once the crane leaves, it will not return". By convention in the Stanford framework (Chang et al., 2009), the head of the first adverb, *bu*, is the verb *fan* and not its adverb neighbor to the right, *fu*. This sort of error may be considered technical mistakes, rather than genuine misunderstanding of syntactic structure.

Tag	Error rate	Tag	Error rate
VV	28.9%	PN	9.6%
AD	10.0%	CD	7.1%
NR	9.8%	JJ	4.6%

Table 2. POS tags with the highest head selection error rates. The top three tags, CC, AS and SP, were omitted due to small sample size (only 3 each).

Dependency labels. When a wrong head is selected, the label was almost always also wrong. Among those words with the correct head, the accuracy in dependency labeling was 88.6%. Table 3 lists the labels with the lowest accuracy. Three kinds of common mistakes emerged.

The top error involves the indirect object (iobj). All four occurrences in the corpus were misconstrued as direct objects.

The second kind of error was due to unawareness of an implicit copula verb. When a copula exists or is implied, the label between the subject and predicate should be topic (top) rather than (nsubj); and the label between the subject and a noun should be attributive (attr) rather than direct object (dobj). Almost all mistakes with the labels top and attr fell into this category.

Third, as another technical mistake, students often failed to use the label preposition object (pobj), and substituted it with the more common direct object (dobj) instead.

Label	Error rate	Label	Error rate
iobj	100.0%	npadvmod	28.6%
attr	55.0%	nsubj	15.1%
top	50.0%	dobj	12.6%
pobj	35.0%	vmod	6.4%

Table 3. Dependency labels with the highest error rates.

5 Research Assignment

Combining the effort of the whole class, 176 of the 320 poems in the *Three Hundred Tang Poems*, comprising about 5000 characters, had been compiled in a treebank.

As a demonstration of the value of their annotations, a research assignment, with eight questions on various linguistic aspects of the poems, was designed. Before the release of the assignment, two preparatory steps were needed: the instructor edited the students' annotations into a gold version, and imported the gold version onto a web-based interface that allows searching for occurrences of specific dependency relations. The user may specify the relevant child and/or head word, or only their POS, and optionally also the dependency label.

Most questions in the assignment required searching for particular dependency relations and observing the word usage therein. For example, students were to find compound nouns where the head noun is modified by the characters "spring" or "autumn", two seasons that appear frequently in formulaic expressions to convey atmosphere (e.g., "wind in the spring", "moon in the autumn"). They were then to recognize the head nouns attested to be modified by both ("grass", "sun" and "light"). As another example, students were to identify all sentences where the usual SVO order had undergone word inversion, and comment on those words that were intentionally given the emphasis. Other questions addressed pivot constructions and onomatopoeia words. Average student performance on these questions ranges between 70% and 90%.

Perhaps the most challenging question was on the phenomenon of parallelism. Classical Chinese poems are read in pairs of two lines, or *couplets*. The two lines in a couplet are expected to have similar syntactic structures, yet the nature and extent of this "similarity" remained an open question. Taking 16 couplets from the treebank as samples, students were to explain any dissymmetry in the pairs of dependency trees, and point out the most frequent differences. About 50% of the students offered ideas similar to the conclusions of a larger-scale study (Lee & Kong, in submission), i.e., that certain sets of POS tags may be considered acceptable as parallel (e.g., numbers and adjectives), and that low-level syntactic structures need not be identical.

6 Discussions and Conclusions

We have described an undergraduate course on language information technology where students collectively created a treebank, then applied it in a research assignment.

This course design is demanding for the instructor, who must correct a substantial amount of annotations, under time pressure to produce a gold version for use in the assignment. Moreover, assignment questions may need to be adjusted, since the annotation results are not available beforehand. It is also demanding for students, who must master the dependency annotation scheme quickly.

The rewards of this design, however, are manifold for students, instructor and scholarship. First, annotation errors indicate areas where students' grasp of grammar is weak, and thus informative for language teachers. Second, some annotations reveal alternative syntactic interpretations, never thought of by the instructor, and can contribute to studies on syntactic ambiguities. Third, the resulting treebank can serve as a linguistic resource for all scholars.

Most significantly, the research assignment lets students reap the rewards of the new knowledge they had labored to create, providing a convincing demonstration of the practical value of treebanking. In future versions of the course, we hope to continue building this "cycle of contributing and learning" (Crane et al., 2012), where students learn to contribute new knowledge, and share it with others so they can collectively discover yet more knowledge.

Acknowledgments

This work was partially supported by a grant from the Early Career Scheme of the General Research Fund (#9041849) from the Research Grants Council of Hong Kong, and by a Teaching Development Grant (#6000349) from City University of Hong Kong.

References

David Bamman and Gregory Crane. 2010. Corpus Linguistics, Treebanks and the Reinvention of Philology. In *Informatik* 2010, pages 542-551.

Emily Bender. 2007. Combining Research and Pedagogy in the Development of a Crosslinguistic Grammar Resource. *Proc. GEAF Workshop*.

Kalina Bontcheva, Hamish Cunningham, Valentin Tablan, Diana Maynard, and Oana Hamza. 2002. Using GATE as an Environment for Teaching NLP. *Proc. Workshop on Effective Tools and Methodologies for Teaching Natural Language Processing and Computational Linguistics*.

Eckhard Bick. 2005. Grammar for Fun: IT-based Grammar Learning with VISL. In: Henriksen, Peter Juel (ed.), *CALL for the Nordic Languages*. pp.49-64.

Pi-Chuan Chang, Huihsin Tseng, Dan Jurafsky, and Christopher Manning. 2009. Discriminative Reordering with Chinese Grammatical Relations Features. *Proc. 3rd Workshop on Syntax and Structure in Statistical Translation*.

Gregory Crane, Bridget Almas, Alison Babeu, Lisa Cerrato, Matthew Harrington, David Bamman, and Harry Diakoff. 2012. Student Researchers, Citizen Scholars and the Trillion Word Library. *Proc. 12th ACM/IEEE-CS Joint Conference on Digital Libraries (JCDL)*.

John Lee. 2012. A Classical Chinese Corpus with Nested Part-of-Speech Tags. *Proc. Workshop on Language Technology for Cultural Heritage, Social Sciences, and Humanities (LaTeCH)*.

John Lee and Yin Hei Kong. 2012. A Dependency Treebank of Classical Chinese Poems. *Proc. Conference of the North American Chapter of the Association for Computational Linguistics (NAACL)*.

John Lee and Tak-sum Wong, 2012. Glimpses of Ancient China from Classical Chinese Poems. *Proc. 24th International Conference on Computational Linguistics (COLING)*.

Martin Volk, Sofia Gustafson-Capková, David Hagstrand, and Heli Uibo. 2005. Teaching Treebanking. In: *Nordisk Sprogteknologi. Nordic Language Technology. Årbog for Nordisk Sprogteknologisk Forskningsprogram 2000-2004*. Museum Tusculanums Forlag. Copenhagen. 2005.

Nianwen Xue, Fei Xia, Fu-Dong Chiou, and Martha Palmer, 2005. The Penn Chinese TreeBank: Phrase Structure Annotation of a Large Corpus. *Natural Language Engineering* 11:pp.207—238.

Learning Computational Linguistics through NLP Evaluation Events: the experience of Russian evaluation initiative

Anastasia Bonch-Osmolovskaya
National Research University
Higher School of Economics
101000, Myasnickaya, 20
Moscow, Russia
abonch@gmail.com

Olga Lyashevskaya
National Research University
Higher School of Economics,
101000, Myasnickaya, 20
Moscow, Russia
olesar@gmail.com

Svetlana Toldova
Moscow State University,
Faculty of Philology
119991, Leninskie Gory,
1 Hum. Bldg., Moscow, Russia
toldova@yandex.ru

Abstract

We present in the paper our experience of involving the students of the department of theoretical and computational linguistics of the Moscow State University into full-cycle activities of preparing and evaluating the results of the NLP Evaluation forums, held in 2010 and 2012 in Russia. The forum of 2010 started as a new initiative and was the first independent evaluation of morphology parsers for Russian in Russia. At the same time the forum campaign has been a source of a successful academic course which resulted in a close-knit student team, strong enough to implement the two-year research for the second forum on syntax, held in 2012. The new forum of anaphora (to be held in 2014) is now prepared mostly by students.

1 Introduction

Russian computational linguistics counts more than 50 years history, started with the first MT research in 1955 (Bar-Hilel 1960). Still up to the first decade of the 21 century all the research groups – those, inheriting the Soviet tradition, as well as the new commercial industry labs - existed in a disjoined mode. The absence of the state-of-the-art investigation on the performance of parsers for Russian as well as on the effect of different computational methods for Russian rich morphology impeded the teaching of computational linguistics, making it dilettantish. It's not surprising that the first initiative of the Evaluation forum emerged in the academy. The academic status of the initiative also guaranteed its independence. The complete cycle of the forum in 2010 on morphology, starting with mark-up scheme of the Gold Standard and ending the final paper preparation has served as a basis for a course in computational linguistics with excellent set of tasks for students to carry out. The problem of the first year experience was insufficient communication with all the participants during the forum preparation. This is very important for the pioneer status of the forum and also the educational perspective of the initiative. That's why the two year period of forum preparation has been chosen. The task of the first year is to prepare and hold a round-table open to all the potential participants where the basic decisions on the test collections, tasks, mark-up and evaluation process are made. The task of the second year is the evaluation forum itself and the preparation of an overview paper. Below we will focus on the educational process: we will describe student tasks during the complete cycle of the evaluation forum preparation. The consistent practical aim of the course distinguishes in from most of the courses in computational linguistics (Hearst, 2005; Liddy and McCracken, 2005; Baldridge and Erk, 2008). This is a course in NLP evaluation which, as we believe, gives students very useful theoretical and practical skills of making sound and deliberate decisions during linguistic data analyses. The main idea of the course is to involve students into solving "real-life" expert tasks, and to show them multiple approaches to mark-up and data analysis. We would like to underline that the practical value of the course: students not only do the routine assessment procedure, but analyze the best practices and create the design of the forum. The course is organized as follows: students complete tasks at home and discuss the results at class with two or three instructors. The experienced students may act as instructors also. The class ends by collective presentation at the conference. Students work in small teams of 2 or 3 persons, each team doing its piece of work. All the students have strong background in theoretical linguistics and math, some students have good programming skills. The main stages of the first year are: 1) getting theoretical background 2) first mark-up experience and proto-gold standard 3) feedback from the participants 4) round-table preparation. The second year consists of the following stage: 5) preparing Gold Standard 6) results evaluation 7) final paper preparation. These stages correspond to the four semesters of special courses on NLP, home task activities, hands-on student activities and practice in academic writing. Each of the stage will be discussed below. The corresponding teaching methods are described in a separate section.

2 Background task

The first task students have to complete is to study theoretical background which consists of a) actual evaluation practices b) state of art of Russian NLP systems that can potentially participate in the forum. Primarily students study reports of the main evaluation forums that have been held on the current task. The topics to be discussed in class are: the types of system running the competitions (statistical, rule-based, hybrid), their theoretical linguistic basis: for example, HPSG parsers or dependency parsers for syntax; the test collections, their sources, size and mark-up scheme; the tasks and their metrics; the performance rate. The students have to find the answers on all this questions making their way through exhaustive reports, they have to draw out some common grounds to be compared and analyzed. For example for the syntax forum (Gareyshina et al., 2012) tree-banks of different languages and structure types has been analyzed and compared. The very important point of this stage is that it results in collective determining some ideal scenario of the future forum which is to be inevitably corrected by performing the second investigation – examining all the information about the potential participants, such as collecting and reading all the related papers, testing demos or installing the open-source resources. For example, the main problem for the morphology forum was to determine a mark-up scheme that would be convenient for all the participants (Lyasevskaya et al., 2010). This problem is crucial because of Russian rich morphology and the variety of theoretical traditions different systems rest upon. The investigation of syntactic parsing (all the systems that took part in the forum, use dependency parsing) revealed the impossibility to compare the types of syntactic relations specified by different systems. The fact is not surprising bearing in mind that there is no open tree-bank such as Penn tree bank to be trained on for Russian. The workshop devoted to comparing different syntactic parsing outputs has been exhausting but fruitful: we arrived to a decision that the main task of the forum should include only evaluating what syntactic heads were to be marked by the participants. Correctness of parsing the whole sentence was decided to count as irrelevant. Only the choice of the head was evaluated. We would like to underline that the design and the scenario of the forums are always determined as a result of individual work of student groups together with collective analysis and summing-up conclusions. Finally the last but not the least object of this task is to juxtapose theoretical and computational linguistics: students have to analyze the scope of underlining linguistic phenomena and to compare them with applied realizations in NLP. The more sophisticated linguistic task is in focus, the more interesting topics are raised in class. For example, the examination of different principles of anaphoric resolution this year showed the limits of applied tasks and solutions (particularly in discourse anaphora resolution and identifying lexical coherence determined extralinguistically), and revealed the perspectives of future development in NLP and artificial intelligence. The analysis is then partly fulfilled in Gold Standard mark-up. The scheme is always broader then it has to be for the evaluation task. The important additional outcome of such corpus mark-up is to prepare some new open resource that can serve also for corpus linguistic and theoretical linguistic research.

3 First mark-up experience and first feedback

As it has been noted earlier the theoretical stage of the course results in the forum scenario and the mark-up scheme for the Gold Standard. At the next stage students begin by making mark-up on a few selected texts. Each text is marked-up with several students and all the cases of interannotator discrepancy have to be analyzed and discussed in class. The discussion leads to formulating more distinct mark-up criteria as well as to determining the cases which should not be evaluated. The mark-up is made by special tool programmed by the students with good programming skills. The specification of requirements for the tool is also the task to be performed by students. The first mark-up staging is all in one testing the mark-up scheme, elaboration of the evaluation framework and metrics as well as technical testing of the tool. As a result some small (usually 100 sentences) "pre-gold" standard is made. Then these sentences (both a non-marked and a marked-up variant) are sent to the participants who had by this time made a claim on their participation in the forum. The idea is to get preliminary feedback to control all the previous decisions that have been made about the forum during the theoretical stage of the course. The participants have the possibility to estimate the mark-up scheme and the assessment scheme and present some on-going results of this first small test.

When we receive the first feedback from the participants, we turn to the analysis of the system possible mistakes. Our aim at this stage is not to evaluate the systems but to exclude all cases which are either theoretically unclear (i.e. the head of the conjunction group) or cannot be resolved by the system (a "boy sees the girl with the telescope" problem) or too difficult to unify (i.e. choice of the basic infinitive for Russian aspectual verbal pairs).

All this activities need special clarification: Russian is a so called "poor resource" language. The forum cannot use existing corpora as a training set. This can violate the independence of evaluation results: some of the system had been trained on these corpora while others had not. So the main practice of our evaluation forums is to conduct assessment on a Gold Standard subcorpus which normally includes about 800 randomly selected sentences that have been manually tagged. Meanwhile the routine of manual tagging serves as an important practical exercise for students.

4 The round-table

The closing event of the first year is a round-table, held at the annual conference on computational linguistics "Dialogue" (www.dialogue-21.ru). The presentation is prepared and done mostly by students and contains all the topics that had been worked on during the previous period: all important background, proposals on the forum scenario and the result of the first evaluation experiment. Usually most of the participants take active part in the round-table. This is besides all an exciting experience for students that have an opportunity to make acquaintance with researches from academy and industry, the opportunity that can have far-reaching effect for their future career. After the round table the work on the second part – the evaluation itself begins.

5 The Gold Standard mark-up stage

The Gold Standard preparation stage includes: the final version of annotator instruction work-out, the tool for Gold Standard mark-up choice or creation, Gold Standard annotators disagreement cases discussion, the final version of Gold Standard creation.

For the Syntax and Anaphora forum the special tools were created for Gold Standard Mark-up. These tools are suitable for annotators decision comparison (Gareyshina et al., 2012). The design of the tool was a special issue for discussion during the class.

The Gold Standard is tagged manually using the worked-out tagging tool. Each item (word, sentence, text (coreference chain)) is independently tagged by two experts-students, then divergences are discussed, if any, and the common decision is made. Each pair of students is responsible for the common decision in case of discrepancy. The discrepancies in pairs are written out in a special document. The students finally work out the list of problematic cases for the corresponding NLP tasks both from the point of view of theory and practical decisions, e.g. the typical morphological ambiguity cases such as Verbal Adjective vs. Participle for Russian or problems of Syntactic relation direction in case of Numeral-Noun syntactic relation, etc. The cases are discussed during seminars. Thus the annotator instruction is improved. Then the annotation is checked by the third expert (one of the tutors). Such procedure allowed us to achieve three aims. It helped to work out the algorithm for semi-automate annotators' mistakes detection procedure. Then, we wanted to avoid 'overfitting': getting the experts used to common error of the specific system and omitting errors by not noticing them. And last, tagging is supposed to give the experts the basic knowledge about difficult cases and to help them form criteria for evaluating mismatches.

6 The evaluation procedure

The stage of evaluation includes the creation a special tool for systems responses comparison with Gold Standard, the comparison of the output of the parsers to the Gold Standard.

The test sets usually are based on a Treebank used for the development of the parsers. In our case there was no Gold Standard Treebank for Russian and there is no Gold Standard Corpora with coreference mark-up. Moreover each system has its own theoretical and practical decisions due to the final purposes of the system.

The students' activity during this stage includes: the automatic comparison tool creation (this is a task for a "programming-oriented" students), the special editor for system responses comparison creation, the manual procedure of system mismatches with Gold Standard analysis.

The latter is an essential stage for Evaluation. As it was mentioned above there are systems' mismatches that should not be treated as mistakes. Thus this procedure includes the collective decision for a repertory of marks used by the annotators for differentiating cases of mismatches, the mismatches discussion during joint seminars, the mismatches manual assessment. All teams of assessors (two students and a tutor) have their own piece of a Gold Standard Corpora to check. Thus every team faces all kinds of difficulties; this principle provides the united consistent approach to all the types of discrepancies.

7 Teaching Methods and Schedule

The Forum cycle takes one and a half of academic years. Thus we have a series of three Special seminars in one of the NLP fields. Students could take part in all the stages of a Forum or only in one of them. The first part is mainly theoretical. They deepen their knowledge in theoretical approaches to linguistic analysis; get acquainted with the approaches to the corresponding NLP task. The other useful activities is a NLP software testing, the real systems discrepancy analysis. The course is also good opportunity to train academic reading skill. The comparison of systems outputs and the work out of Forum parameters are good hands-on tasks. This course is also a challenge for students to learn out how the theoretical principles interact with practical system requirements.

The second course is a practical one. Its primary aim is to work out and annotate the Gold Standard Corpus. Thus this activity could be treated as a series of hands-on in classroom together with exhaustive home-tasks. The course is a project work in a team where IT-oriented students and linguistically-oriented students work together. The practical result is an opened resource such as Syntax Treebank consisting of 800 sentences manually tagged. One of the important educational outputs of the seminar is the acquaintance with the repertory of the problematic cases in a certain NLP field of study.

The Third course is also practical one. Besides the practical tasks of Systems mismatches evaluation this course also allows students to improve their Academic writing skills. The output of this course is not only the Systems evaluation as it is but a scientific article describing the whole Forum procedure as well.

8 Conclusions

The described above students activity as the organizers of the Evaluation Forum, annotators and assessors has challenges for NLP education the enumerated below.

The «outputs» for theoretical stage are the following:

- the high-targeted, and thus highly motivated and deep acquaintance with the approaches to the NLP tasks, existing resources in other languages, methods of evaluation;
- the academic reading skills in NLP research field;
- the acquaintance with the different principle of adaptation the linguistic theory to the NLP task implementation.

The practical-skill training output:

- the annotation skill
- the academic reading and writing skill
- the NLP evaluation skill
- the inter-discipline team-working.

As it has been mentioned, ironically, the resource poverty is a challenge for NLP education with Russian language in focus. At start the procedure of a particular NLP evaluation task for Russian is a terra incognita. Before the Forum starts the number and entry list of participants (and thus the competing technologies) are not predictable. Doing something, that nobody has done before, is always a superb motivation for student involvement.

References

Baldridge, Jason, and Katrin Erk. 2008. Teaching computational linguistics to a large, diverse student body: courses, tools, and interdepartmental interaction. *Proceedings of the Third Workshop on Issues in Teaching Computational Linguistics.* P. 1-8. Association for Computational Linguistics Stroudsburg, PA, USA.

Bar-Hillel, Yehoshua. 1960. The present status of automatic translation of languages. Advances in computers 1, no. 1 P. 91-163..

Hearst, Marti. 2005. Teaching applied natural language processing: Triumphs and tribulations. Proceedings of the Second ACL Workshop on Effective Tools and Methodologies for Teaching Natural Language Processing and Computational Linguistics. P. 1-8. Ann Arbor, Michigan, June. Association for Computational Linguistics.

Liddy, Elizabeth D., and Nancy J. McCracken. 2005. Hands-on NLP for an interdisciplinary audience. *Proceedings of the Second ACL Workshop on Effective Tools and Methodologies for Teaching Natural Language Processing and Computational Linguistics.* P. 62-28. Association for Computational Linguistics.

Gareyshina Anastasia, Ionov Maxim, Lyashevskaya Olga, Privoznov Dmitry, Sokolova Elena, Toldova Svetlana. 2012. *RU-EVAL-2012: Evaluating Dependency Parsers for Russian.* Proceedings of COLING 2012: Posters. P. 349-360. URL: http://www.aclweb.org/anthology/C12-2035.

Lasevskaya Olga, Astaf'eva Irina, Bonch-Osmolovska ya Anastasia, Gareyshina Anastasia, Grishina Julia, D'jachkov Vadim, Ionov Maxim, Koroleva Anna, Kudrinsky Maxim, Lityagina Anna, Luchina Elena, Sidorova Evgenia, Toldova Svetlana, Savchuk Svetlana., Koval' Sergej. 2010. Evaluation of the automated text analysis: POS-tagging for Russian. [Morphological Ananlysis Ocenka metodov avtomaticheskogo analiza teksta: morfologicheskije parsery russkogo jazyka.] *Proceedings of the International Conference on Computational Linguistics Dialogue-2010.* P. 318-327.

A Virtual Manipulative for Learning Log-Linear Models

Francis Ferraro and **Jason Eisner**
Department of Computer Science
Johns Hopkins University
Baltimore, MD, USA
{ferraro, jason}@cs.jhu.edu

Abstract

We present an open-source virtual manipulative for conditional log-linear models. This web-based interactive visualization lets the user tune the probabilities of various shapes—which grow and shrink accordingly—by dragging sliders that correspond to feature weights. The visualization displays a regularized training objective; it supports gradient ascent by optionally displaying gradients on the sliders and providing "Step" and "Solve" buttons. The user can sample parameters and datasets of different sizes and compare their own parameters to the truth. Our website, `http://cs.jhu.edu/~jason/tutorials/loglin/`, guides the user through a series of interactive lessons and provides auxiliary readings, explanations, practice problems and resources.

1 Introduction

We argue that if one is going to teach only a single machine learning technique in a computational linguistics course, it should be *conditional log-linear modeling*. Such models are pervasive in natural language processing. They have the form

$$p_{\vec{\theta}}(y \mid x) \propto \exp\left(\vec{\theta} \cdot \vec{f}(x, y)\right), \qquad (1)$$

where $\vec{f}$ extracts a feature vector from context x and outcome $y \in \mathcal{Y}(x)$. The set of possible outcomes $\mathcal{Y}(x)$ might depend on the context x.[1]

We then present an interactive web visualization that guides students through playing with log-linear models and their estimation. This open-source tool, available at `http://cs.jhu.edu/~jason/tutorials/loglin/`, is intended to develop intuitions, so that basic log-linear models can be then taken for granted in future lectures. It can be used near the start of a course, perhaps after introducing probability notation and n-gram models.

We used the tool in our Natural Language Processing (NLP) class and received very positive feedback. Students were excited by it, with some saying the tool helped develop their "physical intuition" for log-linear models. Other test users with no technical background also enjoyed working through the introductory lessons and found that they began to understand the model.

The app includes 18 ready-to-use lessons for individual or small-group study or classroom use. Each lesson, e.g. Figure 1, guides the student to fit a probability model $p_{\vec{\theta}}(y \mid x)$ over some collection $\mathcal{Y}$ of shapes, words, or other images such as parse trees. Each lesson is peppered with questions; students can be asked to answer some of these questions in writing.[2] Ambitious instructors can add new lessons or edit existing ones by writing configuration files (see section 5.3). This is useful for emphasizing specific concepts or applications. Section 8 provides some history and applications of log-linear modeling, as well as assignment ideas.

[1] The model is equivalent to logistic regression when y is a binary variable, that is, when $\mathcal{Y}(x) = \{0, 1\}$.

[2] There are approximately 6 questions per lesson. We found that answering *all* the questions took our students about 2300 words, or just under 23 words per question, which was probably both unreasonable and unnecessary.

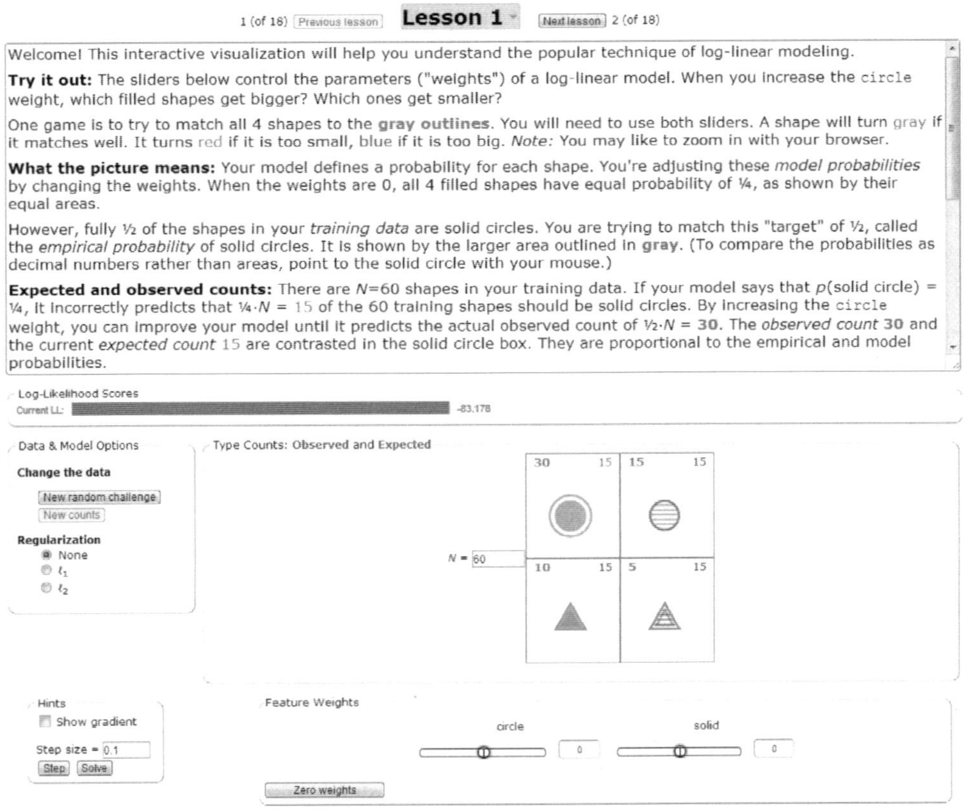

Figure 1: The first lesson; the lower half is larger on the actual application.

2 Why Teach With Log-Linear Models?

Log-linear models are very handy in NLP. They can be used *throughout* a course, when one needs

- a global classifier for an applied task, such as detecting sentiment, topic, spam, or gender;
- a local classifier for structure annotation, such as tags or segment boundaries;
- a local classifier to be applied repeatedly in sequential decision-making;
- a local conditional probability within some generative process, such as an n-gram model, HMM, PCFG, probabilistic FSA or FST, noisy-channel MT model, or Bayes net;
- a global structured prediction method. Here y is a complete structured object such as a tagging, segmentation, parse, alignment, or translation. Then $p(y \mid x)$ is a Markov random field or a conditional random field, depending on whether x is empty or not.

Log-linear models over discrete variables are also sufficiently expressive for an NLP course. Students may experiment freely with adding their own creative model *features* that refer to salient *attributes* or *properties* of the data, since the probability (1) may consider any number of informative features of the (x, y) pair.

How about training? Estimation of the parameter weights $\vec{\theta}$ from a set of fully observed (x, y) pairs is simply a convex optimization problem. Maximizing the regularized conditional log-likelihood

$$F(\vec{\theta}) = \left(\sum_{i=1}^{N} \log p_{\vec{\theta}}(y_i \mid x_i) \right) - C \cdot R(\vec{\theta}) \quad (2)$$

is a simple, uniform training principle that can be used throughout the course. The scaled regularizer $C \cdot R(\vec{\theta})$ prevents overfitting on sparse features. This is arguably more straightforward than the traditional NLP smoothing methods for estimating probabilities from sparse data (Chen and Goodman, 1996), which require applying various *ad hoc* formulas to counts, and which do not generalize well to settings where there is not a natural sequence of backoff models. There exist fast and usable tools that students can use to train their log-linear models, including, among others, MegaM (Daumé III, 2004), and NLTK (Bird et al., 2009).[3]

Formally, log-linear models are a good gateway to a more general understanding of undirected graphical models and the exponential family, including globally normalized joint or conditional distributions over trees and sequences.

One reason that log-linear models are both versatile and pedagogically useful is that they do not just make predictions, but explicitly model *probabilities*. These can be

- combined with other probabilities using the usual rules of probability;
- marginalized at test time to obtain the probability that the outcome y has a particular property (e.g., one can sum over alignments);
- marginalized at training time in the case of incomplete data y (e.g., the training data may not include alignments);
- used to choose among possible decisions by computing their expected loss (risk).

The training procedure also takes a probabilistic view. Equation (2) helps illustrate important statistical principles such as maximum likelihood,[4] regularization (the bias-variance tradeoff), and cross-validation, as well as optimization principles such as gradient ascent.

Log-linear models also provide natural extensions of commonly taught NLP methods. For example, under a probabilistic context-free grammar (PCFG),[5] $p(\text{parse tree} \mid \text{sentence})$ is proportional to a product of rule *probabilities*. Simply replacing each rule probability with an arbitrary non-negative *potential*—an exponentiated weight, or sum of weights of features of that rule—gives an instance of (1). The same parsing algorithms still apply without modification, as does the same inside-outside approach to computing the posterior expectation of rule counts and feature counts. Immediate variants include CRF CFGs (Finkel et al., 2008), in which the rule features become position-dependent and sentence-dependent, and log-linear PCFGs (Berg-Kirkpatrick et al., 2010), in which the feature-rich rule potentials are locally renormalized into rule probabilities via (1).

For all these reasons, we recommend log-linear models as one's "go-to" machine learning technique when teaching. Other linear classifiers, such as perceptrons and SVMs, similarly choose y given x based on a linear score $\vec{f} \cdot \vec{\theta}(x, y)$—but these scores have no probabilistic interpretation, and the procedures for training $\vec{\theta}$ are harder to understand or to justify. Thus, they can be taught as variants later on or in another course. Further reading includes (Smith, 2011).

3 The Teaching Challenge

Unfortunately, there is a difficulty with introducing log-linear models early in a course. Once grasped, they seem very simple. But they are not so easy to grasp for a student who has not had any experience with high-dimensional parametric functions, feature design, or statistical estimation. The interaction among the parameters can be bewildering. Log-likelihood, gradient ascent, and overfitting may also be new ideas.

Students who lack intuitions about these models will fail to follow subsequent lectures. They will also have trouble with homework projects—interpreting the weights learned by their model, and diagnosing problems with their features or their implementation. A student cannot even design appropriate feature sets without understanding how the weights of these features interact to define a distribution. We will discuss some of the necessary intuitions in sections 6 and 7.

We would like equations (1), (2), and the gradient formula to be more than just recipes. The student should regard them as *familiar objects with predictable behavior*. Like computer science, pedagogy proceeds by layering new ideas on top of already-familiar abstractions. A solid understanding of basic log-linear models is prerequisite to

- using them in NLP applications that have their own complexities,
- using them as component distributions within larger probability models or decision rules,
- generalizing the algorithms for working with (1) and (2) to settings where one cannot easily enumerate $\mathcal{Y}$.

[3] A caveat is that generic log-linear training tools will *iterate* over the set $\mathcal{Y}(x)$ in order to maximize (1) and to compute the constant of proportionality in (1) and the gradient of (2). This is impractical when $\mathcal{Y}(x)$ is large, as in language modeling or structured prediction. See Section 8.

[4] Historically, this objective has been regarded as the optimization dual of a maximum entropy problem (Berger et al., 1996), motivating the log-linear form of (2). We have considered adding a maximum entropy view to our manipulative.

[5] Likewise for Markov or hidden Markov models.

4 (Virtual) Manipulatives

Familiar concrete concepts have often been invoked to help develop intuitions about abstract mathematical concepts. Specifically within early math education, *manipulatives*—tactile objects—have been shown to be effective hands-on teaching tools. Examples include Cuisenaire rods for exploring arithmetic concepts like sums, ratios, and place value, or geoboards for exploring geometric concepts like area and perimeter.[6] The key idea is to ground and link the mathematical *language* to a well-known *physical object* that can be inspected and manipulated. For more, see the classic and recent analyses from Sowell (1989) and Carbonneau et al. (2013).

Research has shown concrete manipulatives to be effective, but practical widespread use of them presents certain problems, including procurement of necessary materials, replicability, and applicability to certain groups of students and to concepts that have no simple physical realization. These issues have spurred interest over the past two decades in *virtual manipulatives* implemented in software, including the creation of the National Library of Virtual Manipulatives.[7] Both Clements and McMillen (1996) and Moyer et al. (2002) provide accessible overviews of virtual manipulatives in early math education. Virtual manipulatives give students the ability to effect changes on a complex system and so learn its underlying properties (Moyer et al., 2002). This last point is particularly relevant to log-linear models.

Members of the NLP and speech communities have previously explored manipulatives and the idea of "learning by doing." Eisner (2002) implemented HMM posterior inference and forward-backward training on a spreadsheet, so that editing the data or initial parameters changed the numerical computations and the resulting graphs. VISPER, an applied educational tool that wrapped various speech technologies, was targeted toward understanding the acoustics and overall recognition pipeline (Nouza et al., 1997). Light et al. (2005) developed web interfaces for a number of core NLP technologies and systems, such as parsers, part-of-speech taggers, and finite-state transducers. Matt Post created a Model 1 stack decoder visualization for a recent machine translation class (Lopez et al., 2013).[8] Most manipulatives/interfaces targeted at NLP have been virtual, but a notable exception is van Halteren (2002), who created a (physical) board game for parsing.

In machine learning, there is a plethora of virtual manipulatives demonstrating central concepts such as decision boundaries and kernel methods.[9] There are also several systems for teaching artificial intelligence: these tend to to involve controlling virtual robots[10] or physical ones (Tokic and Bou Ammar, 2012). Overall, manipulatives for NLP and ML seem to be a successful pedagogical direction that we hope will continue.

Next, we present our main contribution, a virtual manipulative that teaches log-linear models. We ground the models in simple objects such as circles and regular polygons, in order to appeal to the students' physical intuitions. Later lessons can move on from shapes, instead using words or images from a particular application of interest.

5 Our Log-Linear Virtual Manipulative

Figure 1 shows a screenshot of the tool, available at `http://cs.jhu.edu/~jason/tutorials/loglin/`. We encourage you to play with it as you read.

5.1 Student Interface

Successive lessons introduce various challenges or subleties. In each lesson, the user experiments with modeling some given dataset $\mathcal{D}$ using some given set of K features. Dataset: For each context x, the outcomes $y \in \mathcal{Y}(x)$ are displayed as shapes, images or words. Features: For each feature f_i, there is a slider to manipulate θ_i.

Each shape y is sized proportionately to its *model probability* $p_{\vec{\theta}}(y \mid x)$ (equation (1)), so it grows or shrinks as the user changes $\vec{\theta}$. In contrast, the *empirical probability*

$$\tilde{p}(y \mid x) = \frac{c(x,y)}{c(x)} \quad (= \textit{ratio of counts}) \qquad (3)$$

is constant and is shown by a gray outline.

[6] Cuisenaire rods are color-coded blocks with lengths from 1 to 10. A geoboard is a board representing the plane, with pegs at the integral points. A rubber band can be stretched around selected pegs to define a polygon.

[7] `nlvm.usu.edu/en/nav/vlibrary.html` and `enlvm.usu.edu/ma/nav/doc/intro.jsp`

[8] `github.com/mjpost/stack-decoder`

[9] E.g., `http://cs.cmu.edu/~ggordon/SVMs/svm-applet.html`.

[10] E.g., `http://www-inst.eecs.berkeley.edu/~cs188/pacman/pacman.html` and `http://www.cs.rochester.edu/trac/quagents`.

The size and color of y indicate how $p_{\vec{\theta}}(y \mid x)$ compares to this empirical probability (Figure 2). Reinforcing this, the observed count $c(x, y)$ is shown at the upper left of y, while the expected count $c(x) \cdot p_{\vec{\theta}}(y \mid x)$ is shown at the upper right, following the same color scheme (Figure 1).

We begin with globally normalized models (only one context x). For example, the data in Figure 1—30 solid circles, 15 striped circles, 10 solid triangles, and 5 striped triangles—are to be modeled with the two indicator features f_{circle} and f_{solid}. With $\vec{\theta} = 0$ we have the uniform distribution, so the solid circle is contained in its gray outline ($\tilde{p}(\text{solid circle}) > p_{\vec{\theta}}(\text{solid circle})$), the striped triangle contains its gray outline ($\tilde{p}(\text{striped triangle}) < p_{\vec{\theta}}(\text{striped triangle})$), and the striped circle and gray outline are coincident ($\tilde{p}(\text{striped circle}) = p_{\vec{\theta}}(\text{striped circle})$).

A student can try various activities:

In the *outcome matching activity*, the goal is to match the model $p_{\vec{\theta}}$ to $\tilde{p}$. The game is to make all of the outcomes match their corresponding gray outlines in size (and color). The student "wins" once the maximum number of objects turn gray.

In the *feature matching activity*, the goal is to match the expected feature vector $\mathbb{E}_{p_{\vec{\theta}}}[\vec{f}]$ to the observed feature vector $\mathbb{E}_{\tilde{p}}[\vec{f}]$. In Figure 1, the student would seek a model that correctly predicts the total number of circles and the total number of solid objects—even if the specific number of solid circles is predicted wrong. (The predicted and observed counts for a *feature* can easily be found by adding up the displayed counts of individual *outcomes* having that feature. For convenience, they are also displayed in a tooltip on the feature's slider.) This game can always be won, even if the given features are not adequately expressive to succeed at outcome matching on the given dataset.

In the *log-likelihood activity*, the goal is to maximize the log-likelihood. The log-likelihood bar (Figure 1) adapts to changes in $\vec{\theta}$, just like the shapes. The game is to make the bar as long as possible.[11] In later lessons, the student instead tries to maximize a *regularized* version of the log-likelihood bar, which is visibly shortened by a penalty for large weights (to prevent overfitting).

Winning any of these games with more complex models becomes difficult or at least tedious, so au-

[11]Once the gradient is introduced in a later lesson, knowing when you have "won" becomes clearer.

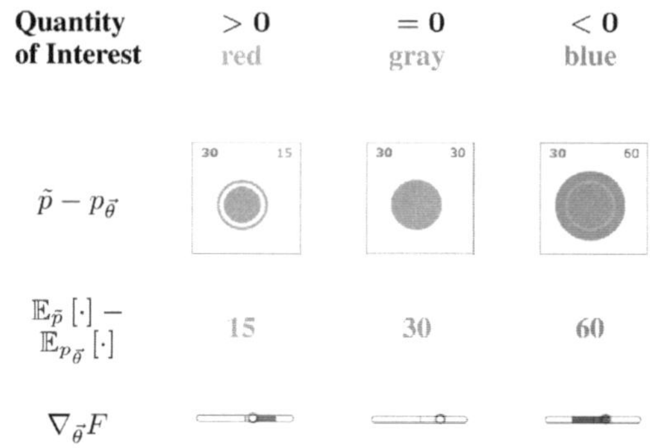

Figure 2: Color and area indicate differences betwen the empirical distribution (gray outline) and model distribution. Red (or blue) indicates a model probability or parameter that should be increased (or decreased) to fit the data.

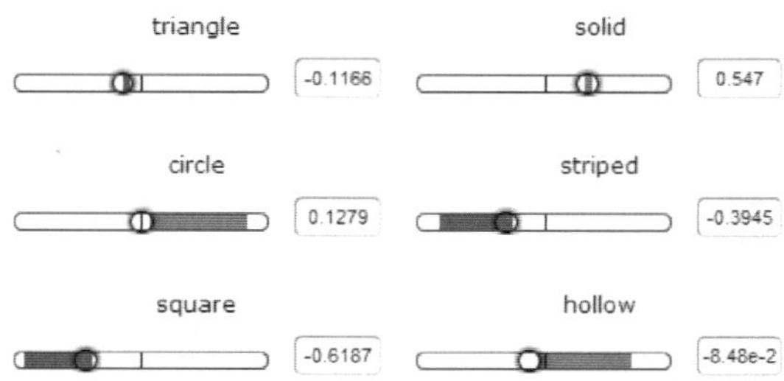

Figure 3: Gradient components use the same color coding as given in Figure 2. The length of each component indicates its potential effect on the objective. Note that the sliders use a nonlinear scale from $-\infty$ to $+\infty$.

tomatic methods come as a relief. The student may view *hints* on the sliders, showing which way each slider should be nudged (Figure 3). These hints correspond to components of the log-likelihood gradient. Further automation is offered by the "Step" button, which automatically nudges all parameters by taking a step of gradient ascent,[12] and even more by the "Solve" button, which steps all the way to the maximum.[13]

Our lessons guide the student to appreciate the relationship among the three activities. First, feature matching is a weaker, attainable version of outcome matching (when outcome matching is

[12]When ℓ_1 regularization is used, the optimal $\vec{\theta}$ often contains many 0 weights, and a step is not permitted to jump over a (possibly optimal) weight of 0. It stops at 0, though if warranted, it can continue past 0 on the next step.

[13]The "Solve" button adapts the stepsize at each step, using a backtracking line search with the Armijo condition. This ensures convergence.

possible it certainly achieves feature matching as well). Second, feature matching is equivalent to maximizing the (unregularized) log-likelihood. Thus the mismatch is 0 iff the gradient of log-likelihood is 0. In fact, the mismatch equals the gradient even when they are *not* 0! Thus, dragging the sliders in the direction of the gradient hints can be viewed as a correct strategy for *either* the feature matching game *or* the log-likelihood game. This connection shows that the current gradient of log-likelihood can easily be computed by summing up the observed and currently predicted counts of each feature. After understanding this and playing with the "Step" and "Solve" buttons, the student should be able to imagine writing code to train log-linear models.

5.2 Guided Exploration

We expect students to "learn by playing." The user can experiment at any time with the sliders, with gradient ascent and its stepsize, with the type and strength of regularization, and with the size of the dataset. The user can also sample new data or new parameters, and can peek at the true parameters. These options are described further in Section 7.

We encourage experimentation by providing *tooltips* that appear whenever a student hovers the mouse pointer over a element of the GUI. Tooltips provide guidance about whatever the student is looking at *right then*. Some are static explanations (e.g., what does this gray bar represent?). Others dynamically update with changes to the parameters (e.g., the tooltips on the feature sliders show the observed and expected counts of that feature).

Students see the tooltips repeatedly, which can help them absorb and reinforce concepts over an extended period of time. Students who like to learn by browsing and experimenting can point to various tooltips and get a sense of how the different concepts fit together. Some tooltips explicitly refer to one another, linking GUI elements such as the training objective, the regularization choices, and the gradient.

Though the user is welcome to play, we also provide some guidance. Each lesson displays instructions that explain the current dataset, justify modeling choices, introduce new functionality, lead the user through a few activities, and ask lesson-specific questions. The first lesson also links to a handout with a more formal textbook-style treatment. The last lesson links to further reading and exercises.

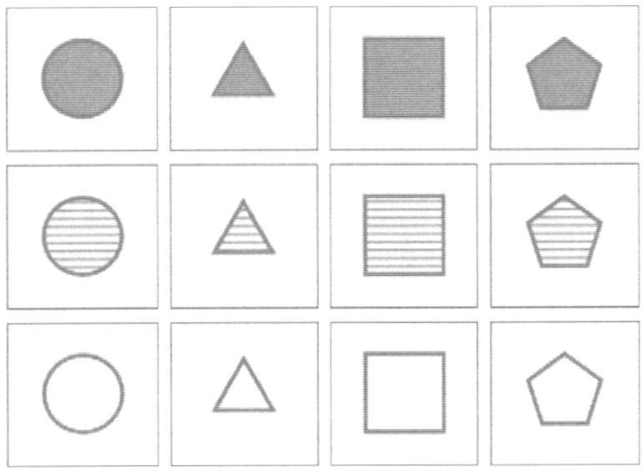

Figure 4: Inventory of available shapes (circle/triangle/square/pentagon) and fills (solid/striped/hollow). Text and arbitrary images may be used instead of shapes. Color and size are reserved to indicate how the current model's predictions of outcome counts or feature counts compare to the empirical values—see Figure 2.

5.3 Instructor Interface: Creating and Tailoring Lessons

An instructor may optionally wish to tailor lessons to his or her students' needs, interests, and abilities. Shapes provide a nice introduction to log-linear models, but eventually NLP students will want to think about NLP problems, whereas vision students will want to think about vision problems. Thus, we have designed the manipulative to handle text and arbitrary images, as well as the 12 shape-fill combinations shown in Figure 4.

Tailoring lessons to the students' needs is as simple as editing a couple of text files. These must specify (1) a set of features, (2) a set of contexts,[14] and (3) for each context, a set of featurized events, including counts and visual positions. This simple format allows one to describe some rather involved models. Some of the features may be "hidden" from the student, thereby allowing the student to experience model mismatch. Note that the visual positioning information is pedagogically important: aligning objects by orthogonal descriptions can make feature contrasts stand out more, e.g., circles vs. triangles or solid vs. striped.

The configuration files can turn off certain features on a per-lesson basis (without program-

[14]The set of contexts may be omitted when there is only one context (i.e., an unconditioned model).

ming). This is useful for, e.g., hiding the "Solve" button in early lessons, adding new tooltips, or specializing the existing tooltips on a per-lesson basis.

However, being a manipulative rather than a tutoring system, our software does not monitor the user's progress through a lesson and provide guidance via lesson-specific hints, warnings, questions, or feedback. (The software is open-source, so others are free to extend it in this way.)

5.4 Back-End Implementation

Anyone can use our virtual manipulative simply by visiting its website. There is no start-up cost. Aside from reading the data, model and instructions from the web server, it is fully client-side. The Javascript back-end uses common and well-supported open-source libraries that provide a consistent experience across browsers.[15] The manipulative relies on certain capabilities from the HTML5 standard. Not all browsers in current use support these capabilities, notably Internet Explorer 9 and under. The tool works with recent versions of Firefox, Chrome and Safari.

6 Pedagogical Aims

6.1 Modeling and Estimation

When faced with a dataset $\mathcal{D}$ of (x, y) pairs, one often hopes to **choose an appropriate model**. When are log-linear models appropriate? Why does their hypothesis space include the uniform distribution? For what feature sets does it include *every* distribution?

One should also understand statistical **estimation**. How do the features interact? When estimating their weights, can raising one weight alter or reverse the desired changes to other weights? How can parameter estimation go wrong statistically (overfitting, perhaps driving parameters to $\pm\infty$)? What might happen if we have a very large feature set? Can we design regularized estimators that prevent overfitting (the bias-variance tradeoff)? What is the effect of the regularization constant on small and large datasets? On rare and frequent contexts? On rare and frequent features? On useful features (including features that always or never fire) and useless ones?

[15]Specifically and in order, `d3` (`d3js.org/`), `jQuery` (`jquery.com/`), `jQuery UI` (`jqueryui.com`), `jQuery Tools` (`jquerytools.org/`), and `qTip` (`craigsworks.com/projects/qtip/`).

Finally, one is responsible for **feature design**. Which features usefully distinguish among the events? How do non-binary features work and when are they appropriate? When can a feature safely be omitted because it provides no additional modeling power? How does the choice of features affect generalization, particularly if the objective is regularized? In particular, how do shared features and backoff features allow a model to generalize to novel contexts and outcomes (or rare ones)? How do the resulting patterns of generalization relate qualitatively to traditional smoothing techniques in NLP (Chen and Goodman, 1996)?

6.2 Training Algorithm

We also aim to convey intuitions about a specific training algorithm. We use the regularized conditional log-likelihood (2) to define the goodness of a parameter vector $\vec{\theta}$. The best choice is then the $\vec{\theta}$ that solves equation (4):

$$0 = \nabla_{\vec{\theta}} F = \mathbb{E}_{\tilde{p}}\left[\vec{f}(X,Y)\right] - \mathbb{E}_{p_{\vec{\theta}}}\left[\vec{f}(X,Y)\right] - C\nabla_{\vec{\theta}} R(\vec{\theta}) \tag{4}$$

where because our model is conditional, $p_{\vec{\theta}}(x, y)$ denotes the hybrid distribution $\tilde{p}(x) \cdot p_{\vec{\theta}}(y \mid x)$.

Many important concepts are visible in (2) and (4). As discussed earlier, (4) includes the **difference between observed and expected feature counts**,

$$\mathbb{E}_{\tilde{p}}\left[\vec{f}(X,Y)\right] - \mathbb{E}_{p_{\vec{\theta}}}\left[\vec{f}(X,Y)\right]. \tag{5}$$

Students must internalize this concept and the meaning of the two counts above. This prepares them to understand the extension to structured prediction, where these counts can be more difficult to compute (see Section 8). It also prepares them to generalize to training latent-variable models (Petrov and Klein, 2008). In that setting, the observed count can no longer be observed but is replaced by another expectation under the model, conditioned on the partial training data.

(4) also includes a **weight decay** term for regularization. We allow both ℓ_1 and ℓ_2 regularization: $R(\vec{\theta}) = \|\vec{\theta}\|_1$ versus $R(\vec{\theta}) = \|\vec{\theta}\|_2^2$. One can see experimentally that strong ℓ_1 regularization tries to use a few larger weights and leave the rest at 0, while strong ℓ_2 regularization tries to share the work among many smaller weights. One can observe how for a given C, the regularization term is

more important for small datasets, since for larger datasets it is dominated by the log-likelihood.

Once one can compute the gradient, one can "follow" it along the surface, in a way that is guaranteed to increase the convex objective function up to its global maximum. The "Solve" button does this and indeed one can watch the log-likelihood bar continually increase. Yet one should observe what might go wrong here as well. Gradient ascent can oscillate if a *fixed* stepsize is used (by clicking "Step" repeatedly). One may also notice that "Solve" is somewhat slow to converge on some problems, which motivates considering alternative optimization algorithms (Malouf, 2002).

We should note that we are *not* concerned with efficiency issues, e.g., tractably computing the normalizers $Z(x)$. Efficient normalization is a crucial practical ingredient in *using* log-linear models, but our primary concern is to impart a near-physical intuitive understanding of the models themselves. See Section 8 or Smith (2011) for strategies on computing the normalizer.

7 Provided Lessons

In this section we provide an overview of the 18 currently available lessons. (Of course, you can work through the lessons yourself for further details.) "Core" lessons that build intuition precede the "applied" lessons focused on NLP tasks or problems. Instructors should feel especially free to replace or reorder the "applied" lessons.

Core lessons **1–5** provide a basic **introduction** to log-linear modeling, using unconditioned distributions over only four shapes as shown in Figure 1. We begin by matching outcomes using just "circle" and "solid" features. We discover in lesson **2** that it is redundant to add "triangle" and "striped" features. In lesson **3** we encounter a dataset which these features cannot fit, because the shape and fill attributes are not statistically independent. We remedy this in lesson **4** with a conjunctive "striped triangle" feature.

Because outcome matching fails in lesson **3**, lessons **3–4** introduce feature matching and log-likelihood as suitable alternatives. Lesson **5** briefly illustrates a non-binary feature function, "number of sides" (taking values 3, 4, and 5 on triangles, squares, and pentagons). This clarifies the matching of feature counts: here we are trying to predict the total number of sides in the dataset.

Lessons **6–8** focus on **optimization**. They move up to the harder setting of 9 shapes with 6 features, so we tell students how to turn on the gradient "hints" on the sliders. We explain how these hints relate to feature matching and log-likelihood. We invite the students to try using the hints on earlier lessons—and on new random datasets that they can generate by clicking. In Lesson **7**, we introduce the "Step" and "Solve" buttons to help even more with a difficult dataset. Students use all these GUI elements to climb the convex objective and increase the log-likelihood bar.

At this point we introduce **regularization**. Lesson **6** invited students to generate *small* random datasets and observe their high variance and the tendency to overfit them. Lesson **8** gives a more dramatic illustration of overfitting: with no observed pentagons, the solver sends $\theta_{\text{pentagon}} \rightarrow -\infty$ to make $p_{\vec{\theta}}(\text{pentagon}) \rightarrow 0$. We prevent this by adding a regularization penalty, which reserves some probability for pentagons. Striped pentagons turn out to be the least likely pentagons, because stripes were observed to be uncommon on *other* shapes (so $\theta_{\text{striped}} < 0$). Thus we see that our choice of features allows this "smoothing method" to make useful generalizations about novel outcomes.

Lessons **9–10** consider the effect of ℓ_1 versus ℓ_2 regularization, and the competition between the regularizer (scaled by the constant C) and the log-likelihood (scaled by the dataset size N).[16]

Lessons **11–13** introduce **conditional models**, showing how features are shared among three contexts. The third context is unobserved, yet our trained model makes plausible predictions about it. The *conditional* probabilities of unobserved shapes are positive even without regularization, in contrast to the *joint* probabilities in lesson **9**.

We see that a frequent context x generally has more influence on the parameters. But this need not be true if the parameters do not help to distinguish among the particular outcomes $\mathcal{Y}(x)$.

Lessons **14–15** explore feature design in conditional models. We model conditional probabilities of the form $p(\text{fill} \mid \text{shape})$. "Unigram" features can favor certain fills y regardless of the shape. "Bigram" features that look at y and x together can favor different fills for each shape type. We see that features that depend *only* on the shape x cannot distinguish among fills y, and so have no

[16]Clever students may think to try setting $C < 0$, which breaks convexity of the objective function.

effect on the conditional probabilities $p(y \mid x)$.

Lesson **15** illustrates how regularization promotes generalization and feature selection. Once we have a full set of bigram features, the unigram features are redundant. We never have to put a high weight on "solid": we can accomplish the same thing by putting high weights on "solid triangle" and "solid circle" separately. Yet this misses a generalization because it does not predict that "solid" is also likely for pentagons. Fortunately, regularization encourages us to avoid too many high weights. So we prefer to put a single high weight on "solid," and use the "solid triangle" and "solid circle" features only to model smaller shape-specific deviations from that generalization. As a result, we will indeed extrapolate that pentagons tend to be solid as well.

Lesson **16** begins the application-driven lessons:

One lesson builds on the "unigram" and "bigram" concepts to create a "bigram language model"—a model of shape *sequences* over a vocabulary of 9 shapes. A shape's probability depends not only on its attributes but also on the attributes that it shares with the previous shape. What is the probability of a striped square given that the previous shape was also striped, or a square, or a striped square?

We also apply log-linear modeling to the task of text categorization (spam detection). We challenge the students to puzzle out how this model is set up and how to generalize it to three-way categorization. Our contexts in this case are documents—actually very short phrases. Most contexts are seen only once, with an outcome of either "mail" or "spam." Our feature set implements logistic regression (footnote 1): each feature conjoins y = spam with some property of the text x, such as "contains 'parents'," "has boldface," or "mentions money."

Additional linguistic application lessons may be added in the near future—e.g., modeling the relative probability of grammar rules or parse trees.

The final lesson summarizes what has been learned, mentions connections to other ideas in machine learning, and points the student to further resources.

8 Graduating to Real Applications

At the time of writing, 3266 papers in the ACL Anthology mention log-linear models, with 137 using "log-linear," "maximum entropy" or "maxent" in the paper title. These cover a wide range of applications that can be considered in lectures or homework projects.

Early papers may cover the most fundamental applications and the clearest motivation. Conditional log-linear models were first popularized in computational linguistics by a group of researchers associated with the IBM speech and language group, who called them "maximum entropy models," after a principle that can be used to motivate their form (Jaynes, 1957). They applied the method to various binary or multiclass classification problems in NLP, such as prepositional phrase attachment (Ratnaparkhi et al., 1994), text categorization (Nigam et al., 1999), and boundary prediction (Beeferman et al., 1999).

Log-linear models can be also used for structured prediction problems in NLP such as tagging, parsing, chunking, segmentation, and language modeling. A simple strategy is to reduce structured prediction to a sequence of multiclass predictions, which can be individually made with a conditional log-linear model (Ratnaparkhi, 1998). A more fully probabilistic approach—used in the original "maximum entropy" papers—is to use (1) to define the conditional probabilities of the steps in a generative process that gradually produces the structure (Rosenfeld, 1994; Berger et al., 1996).[17] This idea remains popular today and can be used to embed rich distributions into a variety of generative models (Berg-Kirkpatrick et al., 2010). For example, a PCFG that uses richly annotated nonterminals involves a large number of context-free rules. Rather than estimating their probabilities separately, or with traditional backoff smoothing, a better approach is to use (1) to model the probability of all rules given their left-hand sides, based on features that consider attributes of the nonterminals.[18]

The most direct approach to structured prediction is to simply predict the structured output all at once, so that y is a large structured object with many features. This is conceptually natural but means that the normalizer $Z(x)$ involves summing over a large space $\mathcal{Y}(x)$ (footnote 3). One

[17] Even predicting the single next word in a sentence can be broken down into a sequence of binary decisions in this way. This avoids normalizing over the large vocabulary (Mnih and Hinton, 2008).

[18] E.g., case, number, gender, tense, aspect, mood, lexical head. In the case of a terminal rule, the spelling or morphology of the terminal symbol can be considered.

can restrict $\mathcal{Y}(x)$ before training (Johnson et al., 1999). More common is to sum *efficiently* by dynamic programming or sampling, as is typical in linear-chain conditional random fields (Lafferty et al., 2001), whole-sentence language modeling (Rosenfeld et al., 2001), and CRF CFGs (Finkel et al., 2008). This topic is properly deferred until such algorithmic techniques are introduced later in an NLP class, for example in a unit on parsing (see discussion in section 2). We prepare students for it by mentioning this point in our final lesson.[19]

Our final lesson also leads to a web page where we link to log-linear software and to various pencil-and-paper problems, homework projects, and readings that an instructor may consider assigning. We welcome suggested additions to this page.

9 Conclusion

We have introduced an open-source, web-based virtual manipulative for log-linear models. Included with the code are 18 lessons peppered with questions, a handout that gives a formal treatment of the necessary derivations, and auxiliary information including further reading, practice problems, and recommended software. A version is available at `http://cs.jhu.edu/~jason/tutorials/loglin/`.

Acknowledgements We would like to thank the anonymous reviewers for their helpful feedback and suggestions and the entire Fall 2012 Natural Language Processing course at Johns Hopkins.

References

Doug Beeferman, Adam Berger, and John Lafferty. 1999. Statistical models for text segmentation. *Machine Learning*, 34(1–3):177–210.

Taylor Berg-Kirkpatrick, Alexandre Bouchard-Côté, DeNero, John DeNero, and Dan Klein. 2010. Painless unsupervised learning with features. In *Proceedings of NAACL*, June.

Adam L. Berger, Stephen A. Della Pietra, and Vincent J. Della Pietra. 1996. A maximum-entropy approach to natural language processing. *Computational Linguistics*, 22(1):39–71.

[19]This material can also be connected to other topics in machine learning. Dynamic programming and sampling are also used for exact or approximate computation of normalizers in undirected graphical models (Markov random fields or conditional random fields), which are really just log-linear models for structured prediction of tuples.

Steven Bird, Ewan Klein, and Edward Loper. 2009. *Natural Language Processing with Python*. O'Reilly Media.

Kira J. Carbonneau, Scott C. Marley, and James P. Selig. 2013. A meta-analysis of the efficacy of teaching mathematics with concrete manipulatives. *Journal of Educational Psychology*, 105(2):380 – 400.

Stanley Chen and Joshua Goodman. 1996. An empirical study of smoothing techniques. In *Proceedings of ACL*.

Douglas H. Clements and Sue McMillen. 1996. Rethinking "concrete" manipulatives. *Teaching Children Mathematics*, 2(5):pp. 270–279.

Hal Daumé III. 2004. Notes on CG and LM-BFGS optimization of logistic regression. Paper available at `http://pub.hal3.name#daume04cg-bfgs`, implementation available at `http://hal3.name/megam/`, August.

Jason Eisner. 2002. An interactive spreadsheet for teaching the forward-backward algorithm. In Dragomir Radev and Chris Brew, editors, *Proceedings of the ACL Workshop on Effective Tools and Methodologies for Teaching NLP and CL*, pages 10–18, Philadelphia, July.

Jenny Rose Finkel, Alex Kleeman, and Christopher D Manning. 2008. Efficient, feature-based, conditional random field parsing. *Proceedings of ACL-08: HLT*, pages 959–967.

E. T. Jaynes. 1957. Information theory and statistical mechanics. *Physics Reviews*, 106:620–630.

Mark Johnson, Stuart Geman, Stephen Canon, Zhiyi Chi, and Stefan Riezler. 1999. Estimators for stochastic "unification-based" grammars. In *Proceedings of ACL*.

John Lafferty, Andrew McCallum, and Fernando Pereira. 2001. Conditional random fields: Probabilistic models for segmenting and labeling sequence data. In *Proceedings of ICML*.

Marc Light, Robert Arens, and Xin Lu. 2005. Web-based interfaces for natural language processing tools. In *Proceedings of the Second ACL Workshop on Effective Tools and Methodologies for Teaching NLP and CL*, pages 28–31, Ann Arbor, Michigan, June. Association for Computational Linguistics.

Adam Lopez, Matt Post, Chris Callison-Burch, Jonathan Weese, Juri Ganitkevitch, Narges Ahmidi, Olivia Buzek, Leah Hanson, Beenish Jamil, Matthias Lee, et al. 2013. Learning to translate with products of novices: Teaching MT with competitive challenge problems. *Transactions of the ACL (TACL)*, 1.

Robert Malouf. 2002. A comparison of algorithms for maximum entropy parameter estimation. In *Proceedings of CoNLL*, pages 49–55.

Andriy Mnih and Geoffrey Hinton. 2008. A scalable hierarchical distributed language model. In *Proceedings of NIPS*.

Patricia S. Moyer, Johnna J. Bolyard, and Mark A. Spikell. 2002. What are virtual manipulatives? *Teaching Children Mathematics*, 8(6):372–377.

Kamal Nigam, John Lafferty, and Andrew McCallum. 1999. Using maximum entropy for text classification. In *IJCAI-99 Workshop on Machine Learning for Information Filtering*, pages 61–67.

Jan Nouza, Miroslav Holada, and Daniel Hajek. 1997. An educational and experimental workbench for visual processing of speech data. In *Fifth European Conference on Speech Communication and Technology*.

Slav Petrov and Dan Klein. 2008. Sparse multi-scale grammars for discriminative latent variable parsing. In *Proceedings of EMNLP*, pages 867–876, October.

Adwait Ratnaparkhi, Jeff Reynar, and Salim Roukos. 1994. A maximum entropy model for prepositional phrase attachment. In *Proceedings of the ARPA Human Language Technology Workshop*, pages 250–255.

Adwait Ratnaparkhi. 1998. *Maximum Entropy Models for Natural Language Ambiguity Resolution*. Ph.D. thesis, University of Pennsylvania, July.

Ronald Rosenfeld, Stanley F. Chen, and Xiaojin Zhu. 2001. Whole-sentence exponential language models: A vehicle for linguistic-statistical integration. *Computer Speech and Language*, 15(1).

Ronald Rosenfeld. 1994. *Adaptive Statistical Language Modeling: A Maximum Entropy Approach*. Ph.D. thesis, Carnegie Mellon University.

Noah A. Smith. 2011. *Linguistic Structure Prediction*. Synthesis Lectures on Human Language Technologies. Morgan and Claypool, May.

Evelyn J Sowell. 1989. Effects of manipulative materials in mathematics instruction. *Journal for Research in Mathematics Education*, pages 498–505.

Michel Tokic and Haitham Bou Ammar. 2012. Teaching reinforcement learning using a physical robot. In *Proceedings of the ICML Workshop on Teaching Machine Learning*.

Hans van Halteren. 2002. Teaching nlp/cl through games: The case of parsing. In *Proceedings of the ACL Workshop on Effective Tools and Methodologies for Teaching NLP and CL*, pages 1–9, Philadelphia, Pennsylvania, USA, July. Association for Computational Linguistics.

Teaching the Basics of NLP and ML in an Introductory Course to Information Science

Apoorv Agarwal
Department of Computer Science
Columbia University
New York, USA
apoorv@cs.columbia.edu

Abstract

In this paper we discuss our experience of teaching basic Natural Language Processing (NLP) and Machine Learning (ML) in an introductory course to Information Science. We discuss the challenges we faced while incorporating NLP and ML to the curriculum followed by a presentation of how we met these challenges. The overall response (of students) to the inclusion of this new topic to the curriculum has been positive. Students this semester are pursuing NLP/ML projects, formulating their own tasks (some of which are novel and presented towards the end of the paper), collecting and annotating data and building models for their task.

1 Introduction

An introductory course to Information Science has been taught at Columbia University for over a decade. The main goal of the course is to introduce undergraduates at our university to applications of Computer Science. For most students, this is their first course in the Computer Science department. The course has no pre-requisites such as higher mathematics or programming. In fact, through a survey we found that about 10% of the class did not know the meaning of a programming language.

Traditionally, the computer science applications that have been taught in this course include HTML (creating a website), Spreadsheets, Database Systems, World Wide Web and the Internet, Algorithms and programming in Python. Given the importance of understanding how humans are building *smart* machines and the amount of excitement around Natural Language Processing (NLP) and Machine Learning (ML) applications, we decided to include a social media analysis application – sentiment analysis of Twitter – in the curriculum last year. The overall response to this inclusion has been positive. One outcome of this inclusion is that the students are now able to build basic models for popular NLP applications such as sentiment analysis of Twitter, spam detection of emails, and document classification. But a more significant outcome of this inclusion is that the students seemed to have gained a general idea of how machine learning works, as a result, they find Watson playing Jeopardy! against the humans, and Google's self-driving car less "magical".

There were two main challenges in incorporating an introduction to NLP and ML to the curriculum: (1) we wanted to include this topic without compromising the traditionally covered material, which put a constraint on the number of lectures we could use for introducing NLP and ML and (2) we were required to abstract away from the inherently mathematical jargon used to explain NLP and ML. In this paper we present the way we met these challenges. We present our lecture, homework and examination design that enabled us to get some of the most important ideas of NLP and ML across in one lecture. The students performed exceptionally well on the NLP/ML section of the examination. Moreover, some students are pursuing projects related to these topics formulating their own tasks, collecting and annotating data, and building models to answer their hypotheses. These are signs that undergraduates with a broad spectrum of educational backgrounds and interests are not only capable of tackling the basics of NLP and ML, but that they may even be doing so with relish.

There has been successful and fruitful effort by researchers in the NLP community to share their experiences and course design through this workshop in the past (Lee, 2002; Eisner, 2002; Liddy and McCracken, 2005; Freedman, 2005; Zinsmeister, 2008). Steven Bird (2008) notes that an introductory course needs to serve some common, basic needs – "For some students, it will be the **first step in a pathway** leading to specialized courses, graduate research, or employment in this field. For students who do not continue, the introductory course will be their **main exposure to the field**. Naturally, this course is also a prime **opportunity to promote the field** to newcomers and encourage them to pursue advanced studies in this area." We share the same motivation (as (Bird, 2008)) – our target audience is in fact "newbies" in Computer Science, who may or may not continue with more advanced topics in Computer Science, in which case this course will be their main exposure to the field and thus offers a great opportunity for us to promote the field.

The rest of the paper is structured as follows: In section 2, we give details of the course and student demographics. Section 3 presents the NLP/ML lecture organization and content. In section 4 we present the problems on the mid term examination and performance of the students on the NLP/ML part of the exam. Section 5 describes some of the most interesting student projects that have come out of the course. We conclude in Section 6.

2 Student demographics

Students enrolling in this introductory course on Information Science come from a wide variety of academic backgrounds. A majority of the class is undergraduates who have never taken any course in the Computer Science department before. The course is taught over a period of 4 months, consisting of 24 lectures of 75 minute duration each.

Figure 1 and Figure 2 present a distribution of 61 students based on their college rank and major (academic background) respectively.

Figure 1 shows that a large majority of students are freshman and sophomores (50%). While these students have an idea of what they would like to major in, they are not required to finalize their majors until the final semester of their sophomore year. This introductory course is therefore a great opportunity to promote the field by exposing the students to some of the most exciting applications of Computer Science. In the first class of the course, we showed the students a video of Watson playing the popular gameshow Jeopardy! against the humans. It was surprising that only a few students knew of Watson. But even the ones who knew about it were excited and curious to learn how Watson actually works.

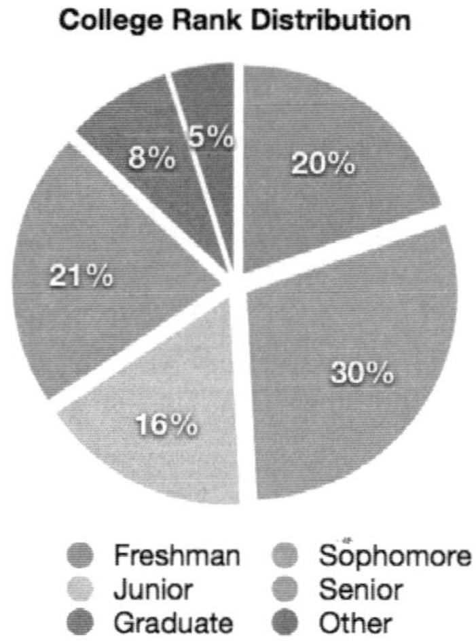

Figure 1: Student distribution based on College rank. 20% Freshman, 30% Sophomore, 16% Junior, 21% Senior, 8% Graduate and 5% Other

Figure 2 presents a distribution of students based on the majors they are pursuing or intend to pursue. For this figure, we grouped the reported majors into the following broader categories: Math/Engineering (Math, Computer Science, Information Science, Electrical Engineering), Basic sciences (Biology, Zoology, Chemistry, Physics, Neuroscience), Political Science, Social Science, Language (German, French, Yiddish, English, Linguistics), Arts and Humanities (including Literature, Film, Theatre), Regional studies (Asian, American, Middle Eastern), and Other (Finance, History, International Relations, Marketing, Philosophy, Psychology).

The distribution of majors shows that the students come from a wide variety of academic backgrounds. Only about 12% of the students are pursuing or intend to pursue a major in Math/Engineering. There is a large majority of students who have only taken

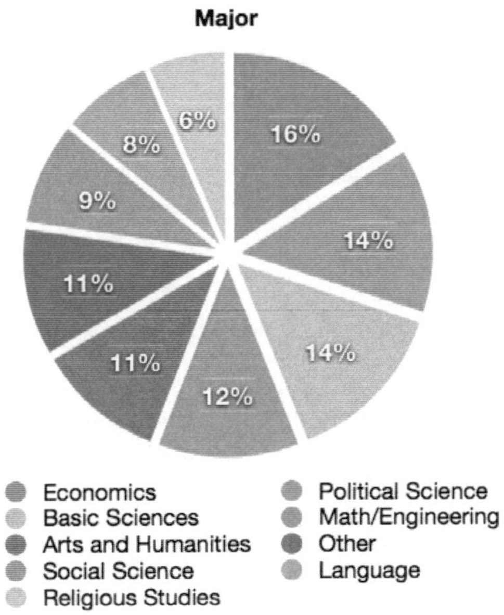

Figure 2: Student distribution based on majors. 16% Economics, 14% Political Science, 14% Basic Sciences, 12% Math/Engineering, 11% Arts and Humanities, 11% Other, 9% Social Science, 8% Language, 6% Regional Studies.

SAT level mathematics. The majority of these students have never used any programming language before. Therefore, one of the main challenges of teaching this course, especially introducing NLP and ML, was to abstract away from mathematical jargon and convey the fundamentals through the use of analogies and concrete illustrations.

3 Lecture organization and content

To meet the aforementioned challenges, we spent one lecture introducing the class to some basic concepts of NLP and ML. Through homework and examination, we introduced the students to more NLP applications that also helped them appreciate the strengths and weaknesses of the simple ML technique we introduced in class. We geared the Python part of course towards text processing preparing the students to implement an end-to-end pipeline of a popular NLP application on another homework.

We started the lecture by introducing a concrete and motivating NLP application – sentiment analysis of Twitter. In line with Reva Freedman's (2005) observation, we found that starting with a concrete application is important. We first defined sentiment analysis as the task of building a machine that is able classify the *polarity* of *opinions* in text into one of two categories: positive and negative.[1] We motivated this application by briefly discussing some of its use cases: predicting the outcome of a presidential election, gauging how a company or a product of a company is performing in the market, finding on average *how people are feeling* based on gender, location, age and weather.[2]

After posing the question – *how would a machine learn to predict if a tweet has a positive or a negative sentiment* – we first drew an analogy of how humans learn new concepts. Humans learn through examples and counter-examples. When we see a new object or learn a new concept, our instinct is to compare the new with the familiar. Our first attempt is to find similarities and dissimilarities between this new object with the objects we have already seen. Similarly, to *train* a machine, we first need to provide it with some *labeled examples*. For the task at hand, *examples* are tweets and their *labels* are manually annotated sentiment polarity (positive or negative). Using these training examples, the machine *learns* patterns of words that signify a particular sentiment.

We started with a small list of words, calling them "features". The training data and features are presented in Table 1. We asked the students to fill out each cell in Table 1 by putting a 1 if a tweet contains a particular word and 0 if it does not contain that word. We mentioned that this process is called "feature extraction", in which we convert unstructured data into a structured representation. This representation is structured because each tweet is represented as an ordered and fixed *list of features*.

We asked the students how they would calculate the similarity between two tweets. And we got an obvious answer – count the number of words they have in common.

The next question we asked was "how might the machine calculate the similarity using the structured representation?" The answer to this question was less obvious but once we gave them the formula,

[1]We defined the italicized words and gave examples to help students understand the definitions. We intentionally kept the definition of sentiment analysis simple and restricted to classifying polarity of opinions into positive and negative categories.

[2]http://www.wefeelfine.org

Tweet ID	Tweet	good	bad	not	pretty	great	Label
T1	It's a good day :)	1	0	0	0	0	+1
T2	The weather is pretty bad	0	1	0	1	0	-1
T3	Alice is pretty	0	0	0	1	0	+1
T4	Bieber is not all that great	0	0	1	0	1	-1
S1	It is a good day for biking	1	0	0	0	0	?
S2	The situation is not pretty	0	0	1	1	0	?
S3	Such a great show :)	0	0	0	0	1	?

Table 1: Training and test data used in class to illustrate how a machine will learn to predict the polarity of tweets.

the students were able to grasp it quickly. We introduced the formula as a bit-wise multiplication of list of features followed by the summation of the resulting bits.

$$Sim(T,S) = \sum_{i=1}^{d} t_i \times s_i$$

where T, S are tweets, d is the number of features in the list of features, t_i, s_i are the ith bit of tweets T and S respectively.

The next question we asked was given a tweet, whose polarity is unknown (an *unseen* tweet), how might they use the training data to predict its polarity. This was a harder question, and though we did not expect an answer, we posed this question nonetheless to serve as a pause in the lecture and indicate that a key idea was coming.

Before revealing the secret sauce, we made the analogy of how humans would do a similar task. Given two kinds of fish, say sea bass and salmon, the way we would classify a new fish into one of these two categories would be by comparing "features" of the new fish with the features of sea bass and with the features of salmon followed by observing if the new fish is "closer" to sea bass or salmon. Similarly, the machine will compare the list of features of the unseen tweet with the list of features of the positive and the list of features of the negative tweets and compute a *similarity score* that will allow the machine to make a prediction about the polarity of this unseen tweet.

We then introduced the following formula:

$$s = \sum_{i=1}^{N} Sim(T_i, S) \times Label_i$$

where N is the total number of training examples, T_i is the ith training example, S is the test tweet and $Label_i$ is the human annotated polarity of T_i.

The machine uses this score to make a final prediction. If the score is less than or equal to 0, the machine predicts the polarity of the tweet as negative. If the score is greater than 0, the machine predicts the polarity of the tweet as positive.

We illustrated this by working out a few examples of how the machine will go about predicting the polarity of the following unseen tweets:

1. "It is a good day for biking"
2. "The situation is not pretty"
3. "Such a great show :)"

We worked out the first example on the board and asked the students to work out the remaining two on their own. Following is the way in which we worked out the first example on the board.

1. First the machine converts the test tweet S1 = "It is a good day for biking" into the same structured representation as that of the training tweets. The list of features for S1 is [1,0,0,0,0] (see Table 1).
2. Then the machine compares the list of features for S1 with each of the training tweets as follows:
   (a) Comparing the list of features for tweets T1 and S1, the machine finds the bit-wise multiplication of their feature lists $[1,0,0,0] \times [1,0,0,0] = [1,0,0,0]$. Then the machine adds all the bits $1+0+0+0 = 1$. We point out there is only one word in

common between the two tweets (namely "good"). The similarity score between the first training example and the test example $s_1 = 1 \times (+1) = 1$.

(b) Similarly, comparing the feature lists for T2 and S1, we get a similarity score $s_2 = ([0, 1, 0, 1, 0] \times [1, 0, 0, 0, 0]) \times (-1) = 0$

(c) Comparing the feature lists for T3 and S1, we get a similarity score $s_3 = ([0, 0, 0, 1, 0] \times [1, 0, 0, 0, 0]) \times (+1) = 0$

(d) Finally, comparing the feature lists for T4 and S1, we get a similarity score $s_4 = ([0, 0, 1, 0, 0] \times [1, 0, 0, 0, 0]) \times (-1) = 0$

3. Next, the machine adds all the similarity scores together to get an aggregated score for the test tweet $s = s_1 + s_2 + s_3 + s_4 = 1$. Since $s > 0$, the machine predicts this test tweet T1, "It is a good day for biking", has a positive polarity.

Having the students work out the other two examples in class on their own and interacting with their neighbors, they began to see the meaning of pattern recognition. Bringing their attention to Table 1, we pointed out that the word "good" is associated with a positive polarity by virtue of appearing in a positively labeled tweet. The word "pretty" is associated with a *neutral* polarity because it appears both in a positive and in a negative tweet. This means that the machine has learned that it cannot make a prediction simply based on the word "pretty". The test tweet "The situation is not pretty" makes this point explicit. This tweet is classified correctly as negative but only because of the presence of the word "not", which appears in a negative tweet.

In summary, through these worked out examples, we were able to drive home the following points:

1. The machine automatically learns the connotation of words by looking at how often certain words appear in positive and negative tweets.

2. The machine also learns more complex patterns that have to do with the conjunction and disjunction of features.

3. The quality and amount of training data is important – for if the training data fails to encode a substantial number of patterns important for classification, the machine is not going to learn well.

Students asked the following questions, which helped us build on the aforementioned points.[3]

1. Good and great are synonyms. Shouldn't we count them as one feature?

2. Could we create and use a dictionary that lists the prior polarity of commonly used words?

3. If the prediction score for the tweet is high, does that mean we the machine is more confident about the prediction?

4. In this approach, the sequence of words does not matter. But clearly, if "not" does not negate the words containing opinion, then won't the machine learn a wrong pattern?

5. If we have too many negative tweets in our training data (as compared to the positive tweets), then would the machine not be predisposed to predict the polarity of an unseen tweet as negative?

Building on these concepts, we had the students work through an end-to-end example of classifying movie reviews into positive and negative on their homework. What appeared to be a promising machine learning technique in class, seemed to fail for this task. They realized that classifying movie reviews is much harder because of the words used in plot descriptions that mislead the classifier. We used examples from the seminal paper by Peter Turney (2002) for this homework problem.

4 Problem and performance on the Mid term examination

We further built on the fundamentals, by asking the students to classify emails into "important" and "unimportant" by using the same machine learning technique (used for sentiment analysis of Twitter) on their mid term examination. This helped them see that the ML technique learned in class may be used, in general, for other NLP applications. As Heike Zinsmeister (2008) notes, redundancy and iterative re-introduction could be helpful for students,

[3]Questions are reformulated for succinctness and clarity.

we found that by having the students work out different NLP applications using the same ML approach helped them grasp the concepts better and appreciate the strengths and weaknesses of this simple ML approach.

Table 2 presents the training data along with the features. Following are the problems from their midterm examination.

1. Extract features from the emails in the training data, i.e. fill Table 2 with ones and zeros. (5 points)

2. What will be the prediction of the machine for this new incoming email "It is important that you register for this meeting. – your phd advisor". Say if, this is an important email, is the prediction made by your machine correct? (4 + 1 points)

3. What will be the prediction of the machine for this new incoming email "Bill, what up?". Say if, this is an unimportant email, is the prediction made by your machine correct? (4 + 1 points)

4. What is the performance of your current machine learning model on all the test data? (2 points)

5. What other feature(s) will you add to the list of features to improve the performance of your machine learning model? How will this change the prediction of the two incoming emails? What will be the performance of your new model? (3 + (2 + 2) + 1 points)

For problem 5 on the exam, most of the students came up with the answer of adding the words "your" and "advisor" to the list of features. But some students devised more complex features. One student proposed to add the capitalization feature to distinguish between "Bill" and "bill". Another student extended this feature to additionally check if "Bill" is a proper noun or not. The only type of feature we introduced in class was the binary occurrence and non-occurrence of words. It was promising to see the students expand on the preliminary feature set to create novel and more advanced set of features.

The duration of the exam was 75 min and it consisted of 6 extended problems. The first two problems were compulsory and the students were asked to do any two out of the remaining four problems (NLP/ML, Logic Gates, Database Design, Machine Instructions). Each of the remaining four problems was worth 25 points. Table 3 shows their performance on the four problems. The table shows that the students did extremely well on the NLP/ML problem – averaging 20.54 out of 25 with a standard deviation of 4.46. Note, students unanimously attempted the NLP/ML part of the exam – only 2 students scored a zero for this problem as compared to 17, 11 and 23 students, who scored a zero on Logic Gates, Database Design and Machine Instructions respectively.[4]

The performance of students on the mid term examination assured us that they were comfortable with the terminology and the process of machine learning. We decided to build on this foundation by introducing them to basic text processing, indexing, and stemming in the Python part of the course. On their Python homework, they implemented a complete pipeline, starting from creating a vocabulary from the training data, then extracting features, and finally implementing a simple version of the perceptron algorithm to predict sentiment polarity of tweets. The average on this homework was 87.8 out of 115 with about 60% of the students scoring over 100 points.

5 Student project descriptions

The most exciting outcome of including NLP and ML to the course has been that some students have signed up for a course project in their demanding curriculum. For the course project, the students were asked to formulate their own tasks, collect and annotate data and build machine learning models for their tasks. Following are the two most novel task formulations (in students' own language) followed by a list of other projects.[5]

Detecting liberal or conservative biases (Allen Lipson and Tyler H. Dratch): Critics on both sides of the political spectrum often accuse their adversaries of employing biased language to promote

[4]The grading was generous and students were given partial credit for their attempt. Therefore, we approximate the number of students who attempted a problem by counting the number of students who scored a zero on that problem.

[5]The project reports are available at www.cs.columbia.edu/~apoorv/Teaching/ProjectReports

Email ID	Email	meeting	register	unsubscribe	bill	Label
E1	Meeting at 4, hurry! – your advisor.	...	...	...	...	+1
E2	Free event. To register click here. To unsubscribe click here.	...	...	...	...	-1
E3	According to our register, your bill is yet to be paid	...	...	...	...	+1
E4	Register for this useless meeting.	...	...	...	...	-1

Table 2: Structured representation of the training data or examples from which the machine will learn to differentiate between important and unimportant emails.

Problem	Average	Std-dev	Median	Count (Score < 5)	Count (Score == 0)
NLP/ML	20.54	4.46	22	2	2
Logic Gates	16.94	6.48	20	20	17
Database Design	13.63	6.48	14	14	11
Machine Instructions	12.8	6.81	14.5	27	23

Table 3: Distribution of scores for 53 students on problems on the mid term exam. Students were required to do any two out of these four problems. Each problem was worth 25 points. Count (Score < 5) means the number of students out of 53 that scored less than 5 points on a problem. Average, standard deviation and median values exclude students who scored a 0.

an agenda. Nowhere in politics is the usage of language more contentious than in the immigration debate. Conservatives lambast "illegal aliens"; liberals defend "undocumented workers." Liberals promote a "path to citizenship"; conservatives decry "criminal amnesty". But is this bias also present in major news sources, the supposedly impartial sources of society's information? Or are papers like the New York Times and the Wall Street Journal firmly on opposite sides of the immigration debate? We want to put this question to the test. We are constructing a machine learning algorithm to detect liberal or conservative biases on immigration in the New York Times and the Wall Street Journal.

The Bechdel Test (Michelle Adriana Marguer Cheripka and Christopher I. Young): The Bechdel Test is a measure by which it is possible to identify gender bias in fiction. In order to pass the test, the work of fiction must pass three criteria: there must be two main female characters, they must have a conversation, and they must be speaking about something other than a man. Though primarily used in film, the Bechdel test can also be applied to literature. In previous Bechdel experiments, the results indicated traditional, heteronormative pattern. While a text does not necessarily need to be explicitly feminist in order to pass the test, the test itself is an important gauge for the social roles that societies uphold and perpetuate. This particular experiment was created in order to determine if this trend was consistent across mediums. Considering that children's books provide the foundation for a person's interaction with literature, the test could identify patterns that emerge from an early stages of literature and address their future impact.

Some of the other project proposals are as follows: Gim Hong Lee built a sentiment analysis engine to rate a professor based on his/her reviews available on CULPA.info (Columbia Underground Listing of Professor Ability). Xueying (Alice) Lin built a recommendation system for Yelp. She acquired the data-set from kaggle.com.[6] A group of three students (Roni Saporta, Moti Volpo and Michal Schestowitz) experimented with the breast cancer data-set available at the UCI data-repository.[7] They used scikit-learn's[8] implementation of the logistic regression algorithm.

It is heartening to see that students who had very limited (or no) idea about how machines learn at the start of the course are now formulating tasks and at-

[6] http://www.kaggle.com/c/yelp-recruiting

[7] http://archive.ics.uci.edu/ml/

[8] http://scikit-learn.org/stable/

tempting to build their own machine learning models. What they still do not know, we believe, is that they are mapping each document into a finite dimensional feature space and calculating dot products between feature vectors to calculate similarity between documents. While this math vocabulary is probably required to make more progress and dive deeper into NLP and ML, we believe it is not required to convey the essence of pattern recognition.

6 Conclusion

In this paper, we presented a lecture, homework and examination design, through which we were able to get some basic ideas of Natural Language Processing and Machine Learning across to students who came from a wide variety of academic backgrounds, majority of whom did not have an advanced math background. Apart from the challenge of having to abstract away from the inherently mathematical concepts, we faced another challenge at the onset of designing the lecture – we had to deliver the NLP and ML material in one or two lectures so that we do not compromise on the traditionally covered topics.

We believe that the lecture, homework and examination design presented in this paper may be used by lecturers teaching introductory course such as ours or by researchers who are interested in presenting a simplified explanation of NLP and ML to general popular science audiences.

Acknowledgments

We would like to thank Kapil Thadani, Caronae Howell, Kshitij Yadav, Owen Rambow, Meghna Agarwala, Sara Rosenthal, Daniel Bauer and anonymous reviewers for useful comments.

References

Steven Bird. 2008. Defining a core body of knowledge for the introductory computational linguistics curriculum. In *Proceedings of the Third Workshop on Issues in Teaching Computational Linguistics*, pages 27–35, Columbus, Ohio, June. Association for Computational Linguistics.

Jason Eisner. 2002. An interactive spreadsheet for teaching the forward-backward algorithm. In *Proceedings of the ACL-02 Workshop on Effective Tools and Methodologies for Teaching Natural Language Processing and Computational Linguistics*, pages 10–18, Philadelphia, Pennsylvania, USA, July. Association for Computational Linguistics.

Reva Freedman. 2005. Concrete assignments for teaching NLP in an M.S. program. In *Proceedings of the Second ACL Workshop on Effective Tools and Methodologies for Teaching NLP and CL*, pages 37–42, Ann Arbor, Michigan, June. Association for Computational Linguistics.

Lillian Lee. 2002. A non-programming introduction to computer science via nlp,ir,and ai. In *Proceedings of the ACL-02 Workshop on Effective Tools and Methodologies for Teaching Natural Language Processing and Computational Linguistics*, pages 33–38, Philadelphia, Pennsylvania, USA, July. Association for Computational Linguistics.

Elizabeth Liddy and Nancy McCracken. 2005. Hands-on NLP for an interdisciplinary audience. In *Proceedings of the Second ACL Workshop on Effective Tools and Methodologies for Teaching NLP and CL*, pages 62–68, Ann Arbor, Michigan, June. Association for Computational Linguistics.

Peter D. Turney. 2002. Thumbs up or thumbs down? semantic orientation applied to unsupervised classification of reviews. *In the Proceedings of the 40th meeting of Association of Computational Linguisitcs (ACL 2002).*

Heike Zinsmeister. 2008. Freshmen's CL curriculum: The benefits of redundancy. In *Proceedings of the Third Workshop on Issues in Teaching Computational Linguistics*, pages 19–26, Columbus, Ohio, June. Association for Computational Linguistics.

Semantic Technologies in IBM Watson^{TM}

Alfio Gliozzo
IBM Watson Research Center
Yorktown Heights, NY 10598
gliozzo@us.ibm.com

Or Biran
Columbia University
New York, NY 10027
orb@cs.columbia.edu

Siddharth Patwardhan
IBM Watson Research Center
Yorktown Heights, NY 10598
siddharth@us.ibm.com

Kathleen McKeown
Columbia University
New York, NY 10027
kathy@cs.columbia.edu

Abstract

This paper describes a seminar course designed by IBM and Columbia University on the topic of Semantic Technologies, in particular as used in IBM Watson^{TM} — a large scale Question Answering system which famously won at Jeopardy!® against two human grand champions. It was first offered at Columbia University during the 2013 spring semester, and will be offered at other institutions starting in the fall semester. We describe the course's first successful run and its unique features: a class centered around a specific industrial technology; a large-scale class project which student teams can choose to participate in and which serves as the basis for an open source project that will continue to grow each time the course is offered; publishable papers, demos and start-up ideas; evidence that the course can be self-evaluating, which makes it potentially appropriate for an online setting; and a unique model where a large company trains instructors and contributes to creating educational material at no charge to qualifying institutions.

1 Introduction

In 2007, IBM Research took on the grand challenge of building a computer system that can perform well enough on open-domain question answering to compete with champions at the game of Jeopardy! In 2011, the open-domain question answering system dubbed Watson beat the two highest ranked players in a two-game Jeopardy! match. To be successful at Jeopardy!, players must retain enormous amounts of information, must have strong language skills, must be able to understand precisely what is being asked, and must accurately determine the likelihood they know the right answer. Over a four year period, the team at IBM developed the Watson system that competed on Jeopardy! and the underlying DeepQA question answering technology (Ferrucci et al., 2010). Watson played many games of Jeopardy! against celebrated Jeopardy! champions and, in games televised in February 2011, won against the greatest players of all time, Ken Jennings and Brad Rutter.

DeepQA has applications well beyond Jeopardy!, however. DeepQA is a software architecture for analyzing natural language content in both questions and knowledge sources. DeepQA discovers and evaluates potential answers and gathers and scores evidence for those answers in both unstructured sources, such as natural language documents, and structured sources such as relational databases and knowledge bases. Figure 1 presents a high-level view of the DeepQA architecture. DeepQA utilizes a massively parallel, component-based pipeline architecture (Ferrucci, 2012) which uses an extensible set of structured and unstructured content sources as well as a broad range of pluggable search and scoring components that allow integration of many different analytic techniques. Machine Learning techniques are used to learn the weights for each scoring component in order to combine them into a single final score. Watson components include a large variety of state of the art solutions originating in the fields of Natural Language Processing (NLP), Machine Learning (ML), Information Retrieval (IR), Semantic Web and Cloud Computing. IBM is now aggressively investing in turning IBM Watson from a research prototype to an industry level highly adaptable system to be applied in dozens of business ap-

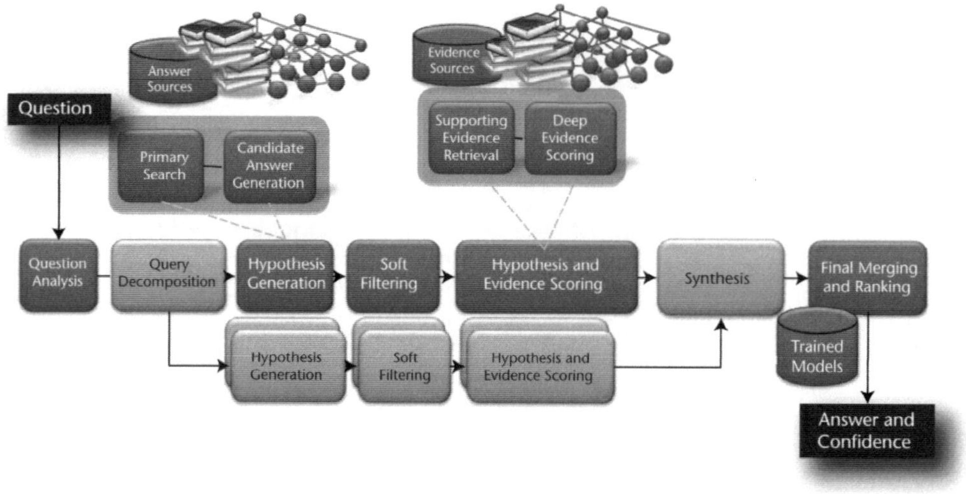

Figure 1: Overview of the DeepQA architecture

plications ranging from healthcare to finance (Ferrucci et al., 2012).

Finding that particular combination of skills in the entry-level job market is hard: in many cases students have some notion of Machine Learning but are not strong in Natural Language Processing; in other cases they have background in Knowledge Management and some of the basics of Semantic Web, but lack an understanding of statistical models and Machine Learning. In most cases semantic integration is not a topic of interest, and so understanding sophisticated platforms like Apache UIMA™ (Ferrucci and Lally, 2004) is a challenge. Learning how to develop the large scale infrastructure and technology needed for IBM Watson prepares students for the real-world challenges of large-scale natural language projects that are common in industry settings and which students have little experience with before graduation.

Of course, IBM is interested in hiring entry-level students as a powerful way of scaling Watson. Therefore, it has resolved to start an educational program focused on these topics. Initially, tutorials were given at scientific conferences (NAACL, ISWC and WWW, among others), universities and summer schools. The great number of attendees (usually in the range of 50 to 150) and strongly positive feedback received from the students was a motivation to transform the didactic material collected so far into a full graduate-level course, which has been offered for the first time at Columbia University. The course (which is described in the rest of this paper) received very positive evaluations from the students and will be used as a template to be replicated by other partner universities in the following year. Our ultimate goal is to develop high quality didactic material for an educational curriculum that can be used by interested universities and professors all over the world.

2 Syllabus and Didactic Material

The syllabus[1] is divided equally between classes specifically on the Watson system, its architecture and technologies used within it, and classes on more general topics that are relevant to these technologies. In particular, background classes on Natural Language Processing; Distributional Semantics; the Semantic Web; Domain Adaptation and the UIMA framework are essential for understanding the Watson system and producing successful projects.

The course at Columbia included four lectures by distinguished guest speakers from IBM, which were advertised to the general Columbia community as open talks. Instead of exams, the course included two workshop-style presentation days: one at the mid term and another at the end of the

[1]The syllabus is accessible on line `http://www.columbia.edu/~ag3366`

course. During these workshops, all student teams gave presentations on their various projects. At the mid-term workshop, teams presented their project idea and timeline, as well as related work and the state-of-the-art of the field. At the final workshop, they presented their completed projects, final results and demos. This workshop was also made open to the Columbia community and in particular to faculty and affiliates interested in start-ups. The workshops will be discussed in further detail in the following sections. The syllabus is briefly detailed here.

- **Introduction: The Jeopardy! Challenge** The motivation behind Watson, the task and its challenges (Prager et al., 2012; Tesauro et al., 2012; Lewis, 2012).
- **The DeepQA Architecture** Chu-Carroll et al. (2012b), Ferrucci (2012), Chu-Carroll et al. (2012a), Lally et al. (2012).
- **Natural Language Processing Background** Pre-processing, tokenization, POS tagging, named entity recognition, syntactic parsing, semantic role labeling, word sense disambiguation, evaluation best practices and metrics.
- **Natural Language Processing in Watson** Murdock et al. (2012a), McCord et al. (2012).
- **Structured Knowledge in Watson** Murdock et al. (2012b), Kalyanpur et al. (2012), Fan et al. (2012).
- **Semantic Web** OWL, RDF, Semantic Web resources.
- **Domain Adaptation** Ferrucci et al. (2012).
- **UIMA** The UIMA framework, Annotators, Types, Descriptors, tools. Hands-on exercise with the class project architecture (Epstein et al., 2012).
- **Midterm Workshop** Presentations of each team's project idea and their research into related work and the state of the art.
- **Distributional Semantics** Miller et al. (2012), Gliozzo and Isabella (2005).
- **Machine Learning and Strategy in Watson**
- **What Watson Tells Us About Cognitive Computing**
- **Final Workshop** Presentations of each team's final project implementation, evaluation, demo and future plans.

3 Watson-like Architecture for Projects

The goal of the class projects was for the students to learn to design and develop language technology components in an environment very similar to IBM's Watson architecture. We provided the students with a plug-in framework for *semantic search*, into which they could integrate their project code. Student projects will be described in the following section. This section details the framework that was made available to the students in order to develop their projects.

Like the Watson system, the project framework for this class was built on top of Apache UIMA (Ferrucci and Lally, 2004)[2] — an open-source software architecture for building applications that handle unstructured information.

The Watson system makes extensive use of UIMA to enable interoperability and scale-out of a large question answering system. The architecture (viz., DeepQA) of Watson (Ferrucci, 2012) defines several high-level "stages" of analysis in the processing pipeline, such as *Question and Topic Analysis*, *Primary Search*, *Candidate Answer Generation*, etc. Segmentation of the system into high-level stages enabled a group of 25 researchers at IBM to independently work on different aspects of the system with little overhead for interoperability and system integration. Each stage of the pipeline clearly defined the inputs and outputs expected of components developed for that particular stage. The researchers needed only to adhere to these input/output requirements for their individual components to easily integrate them into the system. Furthermore, the high-level stages in Watson, enabled massive scale-out of the system through the use of the *asynchronous scaleout* capability of UIMA-AS.

Using the Watson architecture for inspiration, we developed a *semantic search* framework for the class projects. As shown in Figure 2, the framework consists of a UIMA pipeline that has several high-level stages (similar to those of the Watson system):

[2]http://uima.apache.org

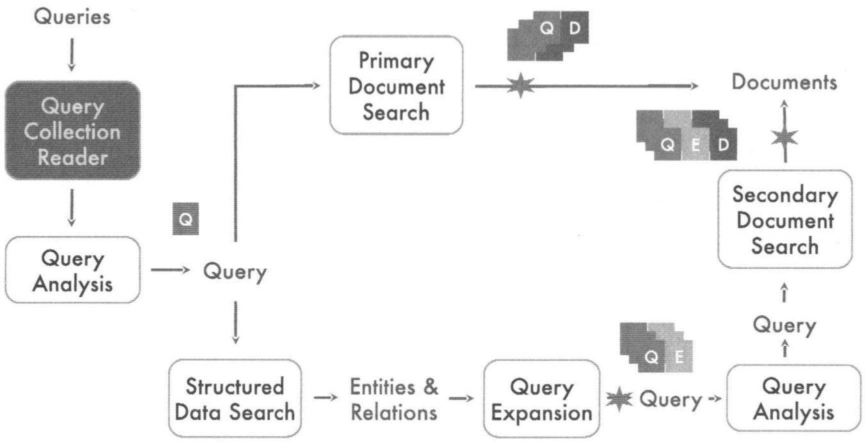

Figure 2: Overview of the class project framework

1. Query Analysis
2. Primary Document Search
3. Structured Data Search
4. Query Expansion
5. Expanded Query Analysis
6. Secondary Document Search

The input to this system is provided by a *Query Collection Reader*, which reads a list of search queries from a text file. The Query Collection Reader is a UIMA "collection reader" that reads the text queries into memory data structures (UIMA CAS structures) — one for each text query. These UIMA CASes flow through the pipeline and are processed by the various processing stages. The processing stages are set up so that new components designed to perform the task of each processing stage can easily be added to the pipeline (or existing components easily modified). The expected inputs and outputs of components in each processing stage are clearly defined, which makes the task of the team building the component simpler: they no longer have to deal with managing data structures and are spared the overhead of converting from and into formats of data exchanged between various components. All of the overhead is handled by UIMA. Furthermore, some of the processing stages generate new CAS structures and the flow of all the UIMA CAS structures through this pipeline is controlled by a "Flow Controller" designed by us for this framework.

The framework was made available to each of the student teams, and their task was to build their project by extending this framework. Even though we built the framework to perform semantic search over a text corpus, many of the teams in this course had projects that went far beyond just semantic search. Our hope was that each team would be able to able independently develop interesting new components for the processing stages of the pipeline, and at the end of the course we would be able to merge the most interesting components to create a single useful application. In the following section, we describe the various projects undertaken by the student teams in the class, while Section 5 discusses the integration of components from student projects and the demo application that resulted from the integrated system.

4 Class Projects

Projects completed for this course fall into three types: scientific projects, where the aim is to produce a publishable paper; integrated projects, where the aim is to create a component that will be integrated into the class open-source project; and independent demo projects, where the aim is to produce an independent working demo/prototype. The following section describes the integrated projects briefly.

4.1 Selected Project Descriptions

As described in section 3, the integrated class project is a system with an architecture which, although greatly simplified, is reminiscent of Watson's. While originally intended to be simply a semantic search tool, some of the student teams created additional components which resulted in a full question answering system. Those projects as well as a few other related ones are described below.

Question Categorization: Using the DBPedia ontology (Bizer et al., 2009) as a semantic type system, this project classifies questions by their answer type. It can be seen as a simplified version of the question categorization system in Watson. The classification is based on a simple bag-of-words approach with a few additional features.

Answer Candidate Ranking: Given the answer type as well as additional features derived by the semantic search component, this project uses regression to rank the candidate answers which themselves come from semantic search.

Twitter Semantic Search: Search in Twitter is difficult due to the huge variations among tweets in lexical terms, spelling and style, and the limited length of the tweets. This project employs LSA (Landauer and Dumais, 1997) to cluster similar tweets and increase search accuracy.

Fine-Grained NER in the Open Domain: This project uses DBPedia's ontology as a type system for named entities of type *Person*. Given results from a standard NER system, it attempts to find the fine-grained classification of each *Person* entity by finding the most similar type. Similarity is computed using traditional distributional methods, using the context of the entity and the contexts of each type, collected from Wikipedia.

News Frame Induction: Working with a large corpus of news data collected by Columbia Newsblaster, this team used the Machine Linking API to tag entities with semantic types. From there, they distributionally collected "frames" prevalent in the news domain such as '[U.S President] meeting with [British Prime Minister]'.

Other projects took on problems such as Sense Induction, NER in the Biomedical domain, Semantic Role Labeling, Semantic Video Search, and a mobile app for Event Search.

5 System Integration and Demonstration

The UIMA-based architecture described in section 3 allows us to achieve a relatively easy integration of different class projects, independently developed by different teams, in a common architecture and expose their functionality with a combined class project demo. The demo is a collaboratively developed semantic search engine which is able to retrieve knowledge from structured data and visualize it for the user in a very concise way. The input is a query; it can be a natural language question or simply a set of keywords. The output is a set of entities and their relations, visualized as an entity graph. Figure 3 shows the results of the current status of our class project demo on the following Jeopardy! question.

> *This nation of 200 million has fought small independence movements like those in Aceh and East Timor.*

The output is a set of DBPedia entities related to the question, grouped by Type (provided by the DBPedia ontology). The correct answer, "*Indonesia*", is among the candidate entities of type Place. Note that only answers of type *Place* and *Agent* have been selected: this is due to the question categorization component, implemented by one of the student teams, that allows us to restrict the generated answer set to those answers having the right types.

The demo will be hosted for one year following the end of the course at `http://watsonclass.no-ip.biz`. Our goal is to incrementally improve this demo, leveraging any new projects developed in future versions of the course, and to build an open source software community involving students taking the course.

6 Evaluation

The course at Columbia drew a relatively large audience. A typical size for a seminar course on a special topic is estimated at 15-20 students, while ours drew 35. The vast majority were Master's students; there were also three PhD students and five undergraduates.

During the student workshops, students were asked to provide grades for each team's presentation and project. After the instructor independently gave his own grades, we looked at the correlation between the average grades given by the students and those give by the instructor. While

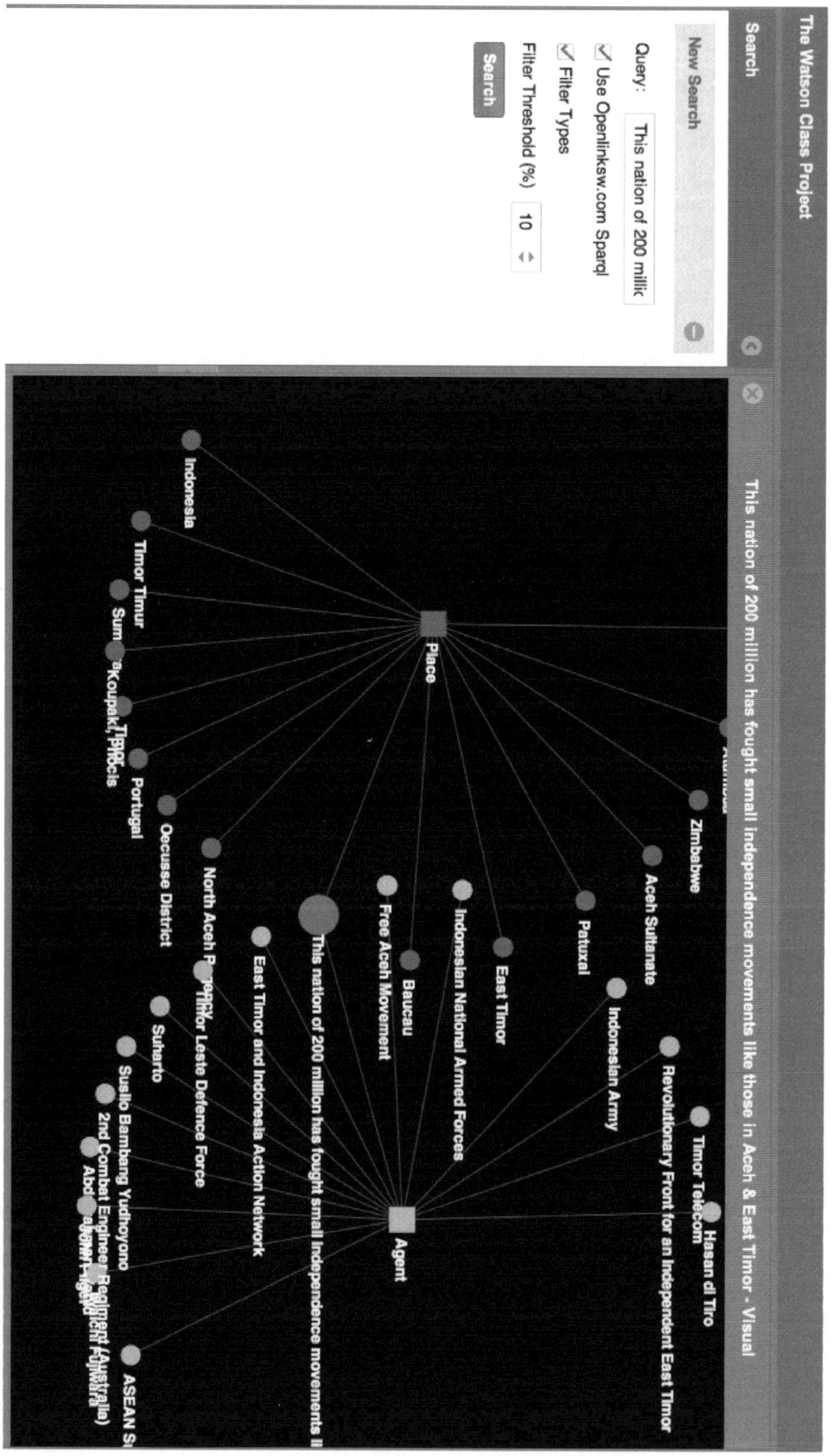

Figure 3: Screenshot of the project demo

Team	1	2	3	4	5	6	7	8	9	10	11
Instructor's grade	B+	B	C+	A-	B-	A+	B	B-	B+	A	B-
TA's grade	B+	B	B	A	B-	A	B-	B+	B+	A	C+
Class' average grade	B/B+	B+/A-	B/B+	A-	B/B+	A-	B+	A-/A	B+/A-	A-/A	B/B+

Table 1: Grades assigned to class projects

the students tended to be more "generous" (their average grade for each team was usually half a grade above the instructor's), the agreement was quite high. Table 1 shows the grades given by the instructor, the teaching assistant and the class average for the midterm workshop.

Feedback about the course from the students was very good. Columbia provides electonic course evaluations to the students which are completely optional. Participation in the evaluation for this course was just under 50% in the midterm evaluation and just over 50% in the final evaluation. The scores (all in the 0-5 range) given by the students in relevant categories were quite high: "Overall Quality" got an average score of 4.23, "Amount Learned" got 4, "Appropriateness of Workload" 4.33 and "Fairness of Grading Process" got 4.42.

The course resulted in multiple papers that are or will soon be under submission, as well as a few projects that may be developed into start-ups. Almost all student teams agreed to share their code in an open source project that is currently being set up, and which will include the current question answering and semantic search system as well as additional side projects.

7 Conclusion

We described a course on the topic of Semantic Technologies and the IBM Watson system, which features a diverse curriculum tied together by its relevance to an exciting, demonstrably successful real-world system. Through a combined architecture inspired by Watson itself, the students get the experience of developing an NLP-heavy component with specifications mandated by the larger architecture, which requires a combination of research and software engineering skills that is common in the industry.

An exciting result of this course is that the class project architecture and many of the student projects are to be maintained as an open source project which the students can, if they choose, continue to be involved with. The repository and community of this project can be expected to grow each time the class is offered. Even after one class, it already contains an impressive semantic search system.

Feedback for this course from the students was excellent, and many teams have achieved their personal goals as stated at the beginning of the semester, including paper submissions, operational web demos and mobile apps.

Our long term goal is to replicate this course in multiple top universities around the world. While IBM does not have enough resources to always do this with its own researchers, it is instead going to provide the content material and the open source code generated so far to other universities, encouraging professors to teach the course themselves. Initially we will work on a pilot phase involving only a restricted number of professors and researchers that are already in collaboration with IBM Research, and eventually (if the positive feedback we have seen so far is repeated in the pilot phase) give access to the same content to a larger group.

References

C. Bizer, J. Lehmann, G. Kobilarov, S. Auer, C. Becker, R. Cyganiak, and S. Hellmann. 2009. DBpedia—Crystallization Point for the Web of Data. *Journal of Web Semantics: Science, Services and Agents on the World Wide Web*, 7(3):154–165, September.

J. Chu-Carroll, J. Fan, B. Boguraev, D. Carmel, D. Sheinwald, and C. Welty. 2012a. Finding Needles in the Haystack: Search and Candidate Generation. *IBM Journal of Research and Development*, 56(3.4):6:1–6:12.

J. Chu-Carroll, J. Fan, N. Schlaefer, and W. Zadrozny. 2012b. Textual Resource Acquisition and Engineering. *IBM Journal of Research and Development*, 56(3.4):4:1–4:11.

E. Epstein, M. Schor, B. Iyer, A. Lally, E. Brown, and J. Cwiklik. 2012. Making Watson Fast. *IBM Journal of Research and Development*, 56(3.4):15:1–15:12.

J. Fan, A. Kalyanpur, D. Gondek, and D. Ferrucci. 2012. Automatic Knowledge Extraction from Documents. *IBM Journal of Research and Development*, 56(3.4):5:1–5:10.

D. Ferrucci and A. Lally. 2004. UIMA: an Architectural Approach to Unstructured Information Processing in the Corporate Research Environment. *Natural Language Engineering*, 10(3-4):327–348.

D. Ferrucci, E. Brown, J. Chu-Carroll, J. Fan, D. Gondek, A. Kalyanpur, A. Lally, J. W. Murdock, E. Nyberg, J. Prager, N. Schlaefer, and C. Welty. 2010. Building Watson: An Overview of the DeepQA project. *AI magazine*, 31(3):59–79.

D. Ferrucci, A. Levas, S. Bagchi, D. Gondek, and E. Mueller. 2012. Watson: Beyond Jeopardy. *Artificial Intelligence (in press)*.

D. Ferrucci. 2012. Introduction to "This is Watson". *IBM Journal of Research and Development*, 56(3.4):1:1–1:15.

A. Gliozzo and T. Isabella. 2005. Semantic Domains in Computational Linguistics. Technical report.

A. Kalyanpur, B. Boguraev, S. Patwardhan, J. W. Murdock, A. Lally, C. Welty, J. Prager, B. Coppola, A. Fokoue-Nkoutche, L. Zhang, Y. Pan, and Z. Qiu. 2012. Structured Data and Inference in DeepQA. *IBM Journal of Research and Development*, 56(3.4):10:1–10:14.

A. Lally, J. Prager, M. McCord, B. Boguraev, S. Patwardhan, J. Fan, P. Fodor, and J. Chu-Carroll. 2012. Question Analysis: How Watson Reads a Clue. *IBM Journal of Research and Development*, 56(3.4):2:1–2:14.

T. Landauer and S. Dumais. 1997. A Solution to Plato's Problem: the Latent Semantic Analysis Theory of Acquisition, Induction and Representation of Knowledge. *Psychological Review*, 104(2):211–240.

B. Lewis. 2012. In the Game: The Interface between Watson and Jeopardy! *IBM Journal of Research and Development*, 56(3.4):17:1–17:6.

M. McCord, J. W. Murdock, and B. Boguraev. 2012. Deep Parsing in Watson. *IBM Journal of Research and Development*, 56(3.4):3:1–3:15.

T. Miller, C. Biemann, T. Zesch, and I. Gurevych. 2012. Using Distributional Similarity for Lexical Expansion in Knowledge-based Word Sense Disambiguation. In *Proceedings of the International Conference on Computational Linguistics*, pages 1781–1796, Mumbai, India, December.

J. W. Murdock, J. Fan, A. Lally, H. Shima, and B. Boguraev. 2012a. Textual Evidence Gathering and Analysis. *IBM Journal of Research and Development*, 56(3.4):8:1–8:14.

J. W. Murdock, A. Kalyanpur, C. Welty, J. Fan, D. Ferrucci, D. Gondek, L. Zhang, and H. Kanayama. 2012b. Typing Candidate Answers Using Type Coercion. *IBM Journal of Research and Development*, 56(3.4):7:1–7:13.

J. Prager, E. Brown, and J. Chu-Carroll. 2012. Special Questions and Techniques. *IBM Journal of Research and Development*, 56(3.4):11:1–11:13.

G. Tesauro, D. Gondek, J. Lenchner, J. Fan, and J. Prager. 2012. Simulation, Learning, and Optimization Techniques in Watson's Game Strategies. *IBM Journal of Research and Development*, 56(3.4):16:1–16:11.

Author Index